NOTTINGHAM FOREST
Miscellany

NOTTINGHAM FOREST
Miscellany

*Forest Trivia,
History, Facts & Stats*

PETE ATTAWAY

NOTTINGHAM FOREST
Miscellany

Published By:
Pitch Publishing (Brighton) Ltd
A2 Yeoman Gate
Yeoman Way
Durrington
BN13 3QZ

Email: info@pitchpublishing.co.uk
Web: www.pitchpublishing.co.uk

First published 2012

13-digit ISBN: 9781908051530

Typesetting and origination by Pitch Publishing.
Printed in India by Replika Press Pvt. Ltd.

INTRODUCTION

When piecing together a haphazard history of one's favourite football club, it helps to have as much history as possible from which to draw. Therefore I count myself fortunate for my birth in Nottingham and my parents' support of Forest which I inherited, as Forest, as a football club at least, have been booting footballs about since 1865, with varying degrees of success.

Of course, when one thinks of Forest, one invariably thinks of Brian Clough, as it was that sorely-missed managerial maverick who miraculously shaped the club briefly into one capable of competing with the best teams in Europe.

Taking nothing away from Old Big 'ed, I've attempted to draw as much from the whole history of NFFC rather than concentrate on those glorious years between 1976 and 1992, just to solidify the notion that Forest didn't just spring into existence the moment BC strode into the City Ground, and vanished once he'd been escorted out after the worse season in his otherwise hugely successful managerial career.

Therefore, you'll read about those founding years on the Forest Recreation Ground, entry into the Football Alliance and the rise to the first trophy, the 1898 FA Cup. You'll read about the fall from grace, those fallow years as a middling second tier side until the fall into the Third Division South in 1949.

How about the re-establishment of Forest as a top flight side under the expert stewardship of Billy Walker and then Johnny Carey, then the brief skid back to the Second Division. Post-Clough, there's the pogoing years from 1993 onwards, right up to the present day and the current man in charge, Sean O'Driscoll. It's nearly always been interesting to be a Forest fan, and I hope this volume succeeds in enlightening the reader as to what an entertaining ride it has been.

Pete Attaway

ACKNOWLEDGEMENTS

As ever, a book is never the work of just one person, even if he is fortunate enough to see only his name on the front cover. For their help, I'd like to thank Ken Smales for his foreword, the NFFC webmaster Geoff Peabody, and again, John Sumpter of JMS Photography for supplying the photos. Thanks also to Paul and Jane at Pitch Publishing. For personal interest and support, I'd like to thank my wife Elaine for another year of suffering a house littered with books and old Forest programmes and memorabilia, and my children Ben, Louise and Brogan. Also thanks as ever to my friends Jack, Jennie, Steve, Holly, Megan, William, Ava, Nevaeh, Kim, Andy, Chris, Sarah, Oumar and Gary for providing me for the necessary distractions so my brain didn't just fill up with random Forest trivia.

FOREWORD

To my knowledge, the first 'serious' book about Nottingham Forest was that written by local sports journalist Arthur Turner to commemorate the club centenary in 1965. Then there was a gap of some 25 years before the next hardback arrived when Pete Attaway, in conjunction with Breedon Books, published *Nottingham Forest – A Complete Record 1865-1991*.

This was the standard Breedon book of match-by-match statistics along with some biographies of well-known players. It so happened that it coincided with the release of my own *Forest – The First 125 Years* of similar concept and that seemed to be the end of publications about the club.

Then Brian Clough's arrival, with his trophy-laden years, spawned an avalanche of books about the club and BC himself, written mainly by professional journalists. Several other authors have tried their hand and a few ex-players produced autobiographies, but after *Who's Who* by Tony Matthews and *How They Gone On* by Peter Gibson, with his book of programme covers recalling memories of past matches, the themes seemed to have dried up – until now.

So here is Pete Attaway's book on what he describes as a hodgepodge of various stories and statistics throughout 150 years or so. Sounds interesting to me.

Ken Smales
Nottingham Forest secretary 1961-1987

THE RECORDS

Record win: 14-0 v Clapton (A), FA Cup first round, 17th Jan1891

Record defeat: 1-9 v Blackburn R (A), Second Division, 10th Apr 1937

Most league points in a season: 94, First Division, 1997/98

Most league goals in a season: 110, Third Division South, 1950/51

Most consecutive league wins: 7, 9th May to 1st Sep 1922

Most consecutive league defeats: 14, 21st March to 27th Sep 1913

Longest unbeaten league run: 42, 26th Nov 1977 to 25th Nov 1978

Longest league run without a win: 17, 25th Oct 2003 to 28th Feb 2004

Record attendance: 49,946 v Manchester U (First Division), 28th Oct 1967

Record gate receipts: £499,099 v Bayern Munich
(Uefa Cup quarter-final second leg), 19th Mar 1996

Transfer fee paid: £4.8m to Celtic for Pierre van Hooijdonk, Mar 1997

Transfer fee received: £8.5m from Liverpool for Stan Collymore, Jun 1995

Most appearances: Bob McKinlay, 685, 1951-69

Most league appearances: Bob McKinlay, 611+3, 1951-69

Most goals: Grenville Morris, 217, 1898-1912

Most league goals: Grenville Morris, 1999, 1898-1912

Highest scorer in a season: Wally Ardron, 36, Third Division (S), 1950/51

Most capped player: Stuart Pearce, 76 (of 78) for England

ANGLO-SCOTTISH CUP WINNERS

Seventeen years before Forest won their first piece of silverware under Brian Clough and Peter Taylor (the Anglo-Scottish Cup) the Reds were involved in a unique two-legged play-off between themselves, as FA Cup holders, and St Mirren, the Scottish Cup holders. Forest played the first leg of this tie at the City Ground, on 23rd September 1959 with a 5.30pm kick-off as these were the days before the ground had adequate floodlighting. Among the St Mirren side was Gerry Baker, brother of future Forest legend Joe, who was at Hibernian at the time. Goals from Tommy Bryceland, Davie Laird and Don Kerrigan gave the Scots a 3-2 victory, with Geoff Vowden scoring both of Forest's goals. The return game at Love Street a week later finished in a 2-2 draw, Stewart Imlach and Billy Gray with a penalty scoring for Forest, Laird and the aforementioned Baker netting for St Mirren, hence handing the Scottish side bragging rights on aggregate. The return game was also the first time Forest had used air transport for travel to a domestic match.

WE ALL 8 BURNLEY

Forest suffered one of their most humiliating defeats ever when, on 21st November 1959, they travelled up to Turf Moor and came back down to earth after suffering an 8-0 loss to the home side. The stars of the show for the Clarets were Irish international Jimmy McIlroy, whose controlling of the midfield had the opposition running after shadows and trying to remember what possession felt like, and emerging striking sensation Jimmy Robson, who stuck five past the Forest custodian "Chick" Thomson. Ray Pointer added two goals for the Clarets, and Brian Pilkington also scored one. Burnley would go on to win the title, while FA Cup-holders Forest endured an unexpected season of struggle.

THE MILLENNIUM GOAL

When inside-forward Johnny Quigley scored the third and final goal of Forest's final match of the 1959/60 season against Newcastle on 23rd April 1960, Forest ended that season having scored exactly 1,000 goals in post-war league football. During the same period, they'd conceded 845. Notably, the game against Newcastle was Quigley's 100th for the club.

HOME, BUT AWAY AS WELL

Most Forest fans will know that Forest played five 'home' league games and one League Cup match at Meadow Lane after the Main Stand fire in 1968, but this wasn't the only time the club used the ground of their near neighbours to fulfil fixtures. The first and only other occasion was on 23rd November 1946 when the River Trent burst its banks and the City Ground pitch lay underneath a couple of feet of water. Rather than hand their players scuba-diving gear, the club asked Notts County to borrow Meadow Lane for the game against Manchester City, one that City won 1-0 thanks mainly to the excellent form of their goalkeeper Frank Swift. Forest have played a total of seven 'home' games at other grounds, and have failed to win a single one of them.

FA CUP FIRSTS

Forest hold a number of 'firsts' when it comes to the FA Cup. They were the first club to reach the semi-final at their first attempt (in 1880). During that run the side met Old Etonians in London and became the first ever provincial side to play an FA Cup tie in the capital. In 1885 Forest played the Glaswegian team Queen's Park at the Merchistone Castle Ground in Edinburgh, the only time a qualifying tie has been played in Scotland, and in 1889 Forest played the Irish side Linfield Athletic, hence becoming the first team to play sides from England, Scotland, Wales and Ireland in the competition.

FOREST REJECT

As Matt Gillies' Forest sank out of the top flight in 1971/72, there could not have been so galling a match for Reds spectators as the penultimate home game of the season, when the visitors were Manchester United. Forest were rock-bottom of the division with three games to go, three points behind Crystal Palace and survival, but all this paled into insignificance when United trotted onto the pitch with recently-departed Forest legend Ian Storey-Moore wearing the number 11 shirt. The 0-0 draw, followed by a defeat at home to Wolves, then a draw at Goodison Park was not enough to ensure safety for the Reds, and their 14-season run of top flight football was at an end.

THE LEGENDARY BILLY WALKER

Forest began 1960/61 in an unusual situation – without Billy Walker in the manager's seat. Walker had managed the club since 1939, seeing them drop to the third tier for the first time in their history (matched by Gary Megson several decades later), then rise back to the top flight for the first time in 33 years. Walker was also in charge when Forest won the FA Cup for the second time overall and for the first time at Wembley in 1959. Walker left the club after grooming a promising crop of youngsters who would go on to hold the side in good stead for the next decade. Everyone associated with Forest were deeply saddened to hear that barely four years into his retirement, Walker had passed away on 28th November 1964, at the age of 67. Walker's successor, the then current Scotland manager Andy Beattie, was appointed on 24th September.

DOING HIS HOMEWORK AT HALF-TIME?

A youthful outside-right became Forest's youngest ever first-class player on 3rd September 1960 when he appeared against Ipswich Town in a reserve fixture aged 15 years, seven months and 19 days despite still being a schoolboy at Mundella Grammar School in Nottingham. The boy in question was David Pleat, who went on to be Forest's youngest-ever first team debutant a year or so later, and who went on to a successful managerial career with the likes of Luton Town and Tottenham Hotspur before returning to the City Ground to undertake a number of varying roles.

500-UP

Jack Burkitt became to first ever Forest player to reach the milestone of 500 league and cup appearances when playing against Wolves on 25th March 1961. His final total of 503 would eventually be surpassed by his long-term defensive partner Bobby McKinlay (who would become the only Forest player to reach 600 games), then subsequently by John Robertson, Ian Bowyer, Stuart Pearce and Steve Chettle. What makes Burkitt's (and McKinlay's) totals so impressive is the fact they largely had only league and FA Cup games to count on, whereas the final four could count European games, the League Cup and a host of minor competitions to add to their totals.

CHAMPIONS!

When Brian Clough-managed Nottingham Forest ascended to the top flight in 1977 after a five-year absence, assistant manager Peter Taylor's bold claim that the club's next ambition was European qualification was dismissed by most commentators as fanciful at the least. A year later, after the crucial additions of Kenny Burns, Peter Shilton, Archie Gemmill and David Needham to the promotion-winning squad, Taylor's claim became reality, as Forest surpassed all reasonable expectations and sat atop the Football League come season's end. It was Forest's first (and so far only) season where they finished on top of the entire league, and beat their previous best showing of a runners-up spot in 1966/67 under the stewardship of Johnny Carey, four points behind Manchester United. The final First Division table of that momentous 1977/78 season is reproduced here:

	P	W	D	L	F	A	Pts
FOREST	42	25	14	3	69	24	64
Liverpool	42	24	9	9	65	34	57
Everton	42	22	11	9	76	45	55
Manchester C	42	20	12	10	74	51	52
Arsenal	42	21	10	11	60	37	52
West Brom	42	18	14	10	62	53	50
Coventry C	42	18	12	12	75	62	48
Aston Villa	42	18	10	14	57	42	46
Leeds U	42	18	10	14	63	53	46
Manchester U	42	16	19	16	67	63	42
Birmingham	42	16	9	17	55	60	41
Derby Co	42	14	13	15	54	59	41
Norwich C	42	11	18	13	52	66	40
Middlesbro'	42	12	15	15	42	54	39
Wolves	42	12	12	18	51	64	36
Chelsea	42	11	14	17	46	69	36
Bristol C	42	11	13	18	49	53	35
Ipswich T	42	11	13	18	47	61	35
QPR	42	9	15	18	47	64	33
West Ham U	42	12	8	22	52	69	32
Newcastle U	42	6	10	26	42	78	22
Leicester C	42	5	12	25	26	79	22

FOREST THE GIANT KILLERS #1

Most Forest fans would assume their team have always more qualified as giants to be slaughtered, not the other way around, but for much of the side's history, that has not been the case. In 1927/28, Forest were a middling Second Division club who embarked on a cup run that saw a pleasing amount of coppers enter the purse. After dealing with Third Division North promotion-chasers Tranmere Rovers in the third round, Forest were drawn against rivals Derby County, who were a top flight side at the time, battling in what was a very even league. After a 0-0 draw at the Baseball Ground on 28th January, Forest brought Derby back to the City Ground four days later and beat them 2-0, the goals coming from Syd Gibson and Cyril Stocks. The Reds' reward was a home draw against Cardiff City. The Bluebirds were seventh in the First Division, five points behind leaders Everton, but they gained no respect from Forest who triumphed 2-1 with goals from Stocks and right-back Billy Thompson. This gave Forest a real chance of their first Wembley final, although they and Stoke City were the only non top flight sides left in the competition. The draw was not favourable though, and Forest were away at Sheffield United. Even though the Blades were in the First Division relegation zone at the time, they proved too powerful and won 3-0, ending the Reds' cup-winning dreams.

NOTTS UNITED

Over the years, a handful of players have played for all three of Nottinghamshire's professional sides: Forest, Notts County and Mansfield Town. Striker Trevor Christie managed it in the 1980s although his stay at Forest was only a brief one, while more recently goalkeeper Darren Ward, centre-half Colin Calderwood, forward Jason Lee and defender John Thompson have all achieved the feat. In 2012 Kieron Freeman made history in uniquely playing for all three Nottinghamshire teams in consecutive matches. He ended a loan spell with Mansfield from Forest with a game against York City on New Year's Day in the Conference, returned to the City Ground and played for Forest in an FA Cup tie against Leicester, then immediately joined Notts County on loan and played in a league game at Bournemouth in League 1. Freeman was only 19, and played each game on successive weekends.

NUMBER ONE IS...

Peter Shilton. Shilton had been coveted by Brian Clough for many years, and was one of the players he planned to sign for Leeds United. He had to wait until September 1977 before he finally employed Shilts, advising the Forest board it would cost £250,000 to get the man he considered the most important piece of his Forest championship jigsaw. At the time, Shilton's career was nose-diving, shot-stopping in the second tier with Stoke City and playing second fiddle to Liverpool's Ray Clemence in the England team. Back in the top flight, and with Forest grabbing the headlines with their steamroller charge towards the title, Shilton rediscovered the form that had initially propelled him into the limelight, firstly as a youngster at Leicester City. Shilton ended the 1977/78 season by winning the PFA Player of the Year award, and of course the title, conceding a miserly 18 goals in his 37 games. He regained his England place, although the manager at the time, Ron Greenwood, maintained his loyalty to Clemence by making him and Shilton take turns in goal. Shilton remained with the Reds throughout their glory years, before deciding a change was in order and leaving for Southampton in the summer of 1982. He eventually became England's undisputed number one, winning a record 125 caps before his retirement from international football after Italia 90. As a player he later served Derby County, Plymouth, Wimbledon, Bolton, Coventry, West Ham and Leyton Orient, the latter with whom he played his 1,000th league game. Despite being at Forest less than four years, there's hardly any doubt Shilts will always be regarded as the greatest keeper to wear Forest's number one jersey.

THE TRANSFER THAT NEVER WAS

Brian Clough, like The Mounties, always got his man – well, not quite. In 1972 Clough announced he had signed Forest's highly-skilled and long-serving outside-left Ian Storey-Moore. Moore was even paraded around the Baseball Ground prior to a Derby league game. However, the transfer forms has not yet been completed – they were missing the signature of Forest secretary Ken Smales, and Forest's number 11 remained up for grabs. In the end, Moore instead signed for Manchester United for £240,000. It wasn't a happy move though as at United two years later Moore suffered a serious leg injury that ended his top flight career.

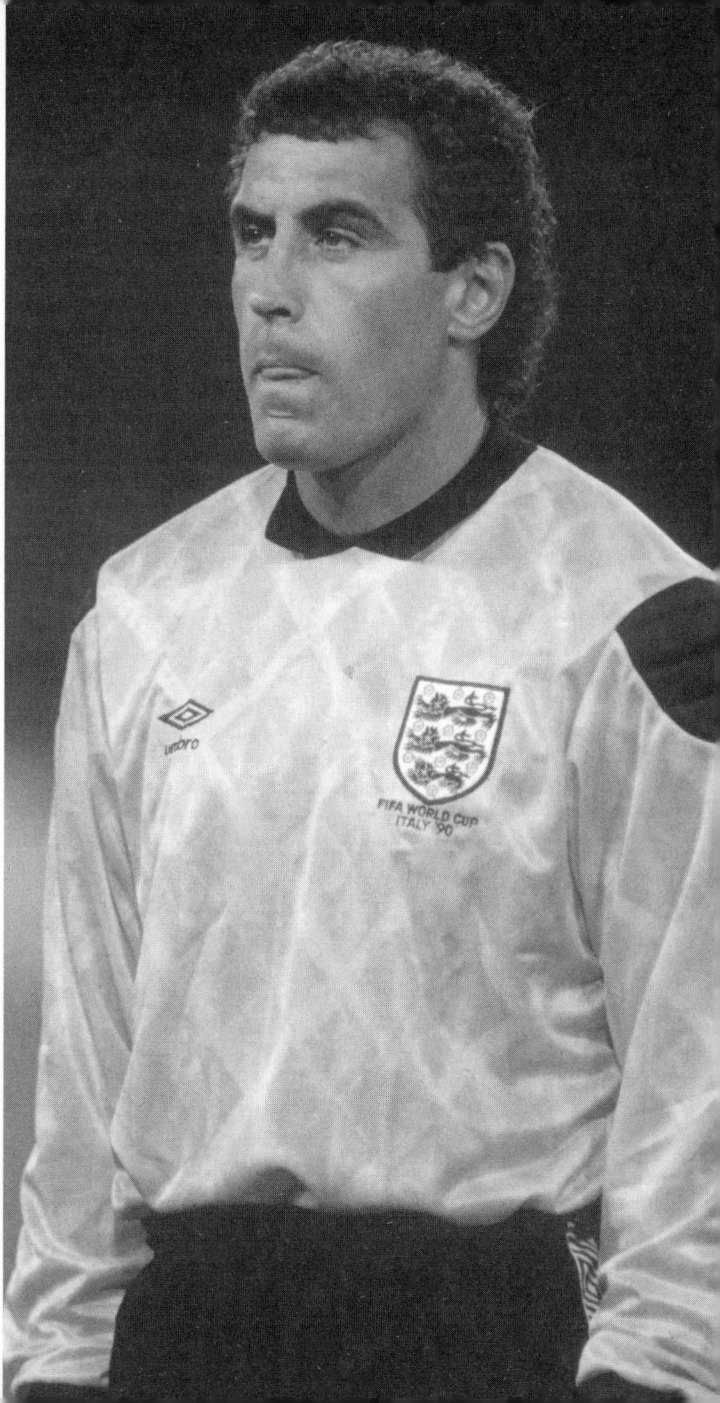

FOREST'S NUMBER ONE OF ALL TIME PETER SHILTON

INTO EUROPE

As anyone knows, Nottingham Forest have won the European Cup twice (in 1979 and 1980), but they took their first strides into European competition long before that in 1961, in the Coupe Internationale des Villes de Foires, the Inter-Cities Fairs Cup as it was known in England. Their first opponents were Spanish side Valencia, who visited on 4th October 1961 for the first leg of the first round. This was also only the second game in Forest's history where they were allowed to name a substitute for the match (the other being the 1959 Charity Shield), although this was a goalkeeper who was only allowed on should the first choice be injured and passed by the referee as unable to continue. Forest lost 2-0 at home, then crashed 5-1 in the return three weeks later, bringing to an abrupt end their first European adventure, whereas Valencia went on to beat Barcelona in the final. Forest applied the following season to take part again, but Everton were chosen instead by the FA to represent England.

FORMAN BROS

Frank and Fred Forman hold a unique place in Forest's history and certainly are the most successful pair of brothers ever to play for the club. Born in Aston-on-Trent in Derbyshire, Fred on 8th November 1873 and Frank on 23rd May 1875, both played their football as youngsters in the Derbyshire area before playing for Beeston Town in Nottinghamshire. Here they were spotted by Derby County who signed them both, inside-forward Fred in 1892 and Frank, a wing-half, in 1894. Forest signed Fred in 1894 and Frank soon after, and they both spent over a decade at the club. In 1899 the pair set a record that was never matched, in being selected for all three of England's home internationals for that season. They were also the first pair of brothers at the same club at the same time to be selected for England, a feat unmatched until 1996 by Manchester United's Gary and Phil Neville. After retiring in 1903, Fred passed away at the early age of 36 in Skegness. Frank returned to Forest in 1935 to join the committee where he served until his death in 1961. To complete the family connection, Frank and Fred's nephew, Harry Linacre, was Forest's custodian for ten years, making over 300 appearances for the side.

SHINN(E)Y NOT SHINTY

The origins of Nottingham Forest stem from two sources – their first home and how the club originally formed. In the 1860s a club came together which played 'shinney' (or 'shinny'), an informal type of hockey that was named due to the frequency of players receiving blows on the shin from opposition sticks. The club was based at Nottingham's Forest Recreation Ground, itself named as it used to form part of Sherwood Forest before developments cut the area off from the rest of the woodland. Around 1865 the shinny club decide to give the developing game of football a try – and enjoyed themselves so much they abandoned their sticks and took up the game full time. They became known as the Forest Football Club, later adding the Nottingham tag, probably to distinguish themselves from the Notts. Football Club, who eventually became Notts County. Forest continued to play their games at the Recreation Ground until 1879. The ancient sport of 'shinn(e)y' is not to be confused with the Gaelic game of 'shinty', which itself is also a form of hockey.

SAM WELLER WIDDOWSON

Of all the players who brought Forest forwards over their early years, perhaps the individual with the most to be thanked for was Sam Weller Widdowson, a fantastic all-round sportsman, later a football referee and Forest chairman between 1879 and 1884. Sam (who is sometimes erroneously referred to as 'Samuel' whereas records exist that prove he was simply christened 'Sam') was born in Hucknall Torkard on 16th April 1851, and was so named after the character Sam Weller in Charles Dickens' *Pickwick Papers*. He played for Forest as a centre-forward and is credited as inventing the 2-3-5 formation that most teams used rigidly for almost 100 years. Most famously of all, Sam displayed his dislike of the tactic of 'hacking' (kicking your opponents' shins) by turning up for one game wearing a pair of cut-down cricket pads. He was instantly ridiculed for his 'unmanliness' but it wasn't long before most players had caught on to the notion of shin-guards and they eventually became required by the laws of the game. For one final first, Widdowson was also the referee for the first official match in which goal nets were used. Sam died in Beeston in May 1927.

THIRD TIER HIGHS AND LOWS

In 1957, Forest set a record in becoming the first team post-war to rise from the Third Division to the top flight, having previously being promoted from the Third Division South in 1950/51. A less delightful record was set by the club in 2005 when Forest were relegated to League 1, hence becoming the first side to have won the European Cup and subsequently be relegated to the third tier of their national league system.

AN ENGLAND XI

A Forest XI made up of players who gained caps for England:

1 Peter Shilton ....(19 caps 1978-82, 125 caps total)
2 Viv Anderson ....(11 caps, 1978-84, 30 caps total)
3 Stuart Pearce ....(76 caps, 1987-97, 78 caps total)
4 Des Walker ....(47 caps, 1988-92, 59 caps total)
5 Larry Lloyd ....(one cap, 1980, four caps total)
6 Steve Hodge ....(nine caps, 1988-91, 24 caps total)
7 Steve Stone ....(nine caps, 1995-96, nine caps total)
8 Neil Webb ....(18 caps, 1987-89, 26 caps total)
9 Garry Birtles ....(three caps, 1980, three caps total)
10 Tony Woodcock ....(eight caps, 1978-79, 42 caps total)
11 Trevor Francis ....(ten caps, 1979-81, 52 caps total)

TOP OF THE POPS

Forest players have smashed into the pop charts on many occasions. Virtually the whole squad turned out to appear on the 1978 monster hit 'We've Got the Whole World in His Hands', a joint effort with local pop legends Paper Lace of 'Billy Don't Be A Hero' fame. It peaked just outside the top 20 in the UK, but reached number one in Holland. Forest players have also appeared on many of the songs released by various home nation squads, particularly England and Scotland, with John Robertson actually receiving a mention in the lyrics of Scotland's 1982 effort We Have a Dream, written by BA Robertson. Brian Clough released 'You Can't Win 'em All' in 1980, a collaboration with J J Barrie, while Peter Shilton and Ray Clemence recorded 'Side by Side' around the same time. Neither of these efforts managed to dent the singles chart.

THE TRENTSIDE DERBY...

...or the Nottingham derby (and not the Nottinghamshire derby, Notts County v Mansfield Town) is the name given to matches between Forest and their closest geographical rivals, Notts County. This match was, until the late 1950s, a seasonal occurrence as Forest and County were equitable in terms of footballing success, but since Billy Walker steered Forest back to the top flight in 1957, a feat County have only briefly matched, games have been few and far between. The first game between 'Forest' and 'Notts.' occurred in 1866 – there are mixed reports of the game, some claiming a 1-0 win for Forest, but the accepted result is now a 0-0 draw, despite Forest having 16 players to Notts' 12. Forest's first FA Cup tie (and first competitive match) was against County, on 16th November 1878, which Forest won 3-1. County gained revenge and won by the same score in 1892 when the clubs first met in the Football League. Up to and including the 2011/12 season the sides had met 94 times in competitive football, with Forest having the upper hand, winning 40 times to County's 30, with 24 draws. Forest hold the record for the biggest winning margin, 5-0, achieved in 1901/02 and 1953/54. County's biggest win is 4-1, recorded in February 1952. There have been only 20 competitive games between the sides since 1957. Forest hammered Notts 4-0 on their way to the 1978 League Cup Final, a surprising scoreline as only six months previously the two sides has been virtually equal rivals in a promotion chase out of the second tier. County currently hold the unofficial title of 'Trentside Derby League Champions' as they won the last time the clubs met in the league, right-back Charlie Palmer scoring in a 2-1 victory with six minutes left as Forest chased promotion to the top flight. The first competitive match for over 17 years occurred in August 2011 when the sides met at the City Ground in the first round of the League Cup. Forest triumphed 4-3 on penalties after a thrilling 3-3 draw secured only when Wes Morgan scored a thumping drive in the 122nd minute. In the shoot-out it was 3-3 again when George Boateng had his spot-kick saved by County's Stuart Nelson. Fortunately for the Reds, the Magpies' Lee Hughes and Neal Bishop both missed theirs, sandwiching Luke Chambers' successful effort.

BRIAN CLOUGH'S LEGACY

Brian Clough may not have been the best manager of all time, but he was certainly in the top one. Here is a list of 25 players who played under the great man at Nottingham Forest, then went on to dip their fingers into managerial territories themselves.

Neil Martin

The journeyman forward, scorer of 100 goals in both England and Scotland, only had a brief spell under Clough at Forest, but did manage to score the Reds' first goal following Old Big 'ed's appointment. Martin's managerial career was also suitably sparse, half a season at the helm at Walsall.

Martin O'Neill

Perhaps the most famous graduate of the Clough School of Management, and indeed the most successful, the former law student spent time in non-league with Grantham, Shepshed and Wycombe before he guided the latter into the league. Then came six months at Norwich before more triumphant spells at Leicester, Celtic and Aston Villa. He took over at Sunderland in December 2011. Notably, whenever Forest's managerial chair is vacated, O'Neill's name seems invariably to crop up in speculation.

Ian Bowyer

A superb Forest servant, Bowyer was released in 1987 after well over 500 games for the club to take over as player-manager of Hereford United. He managed one Welsh Cup in three seasons before leaving in 1990, later coaching at Forest under Paul Hart.

Tony Woodcock

A young striker who didn't seem to make the most of his opportunities until Clough arrived on the scene and polished him into an England international, Woodcock left for Cologne in 1980. Woodcock's sole managerial stint was also in Germany, four months in charge at VfB Leipzig in 1994.

Viv Anderson

The giant-striding full-back known as "Spider" gained eternal fame as

England's first black full international, and spent 1993/94 as player-manager of Barnsley. It was a disappointing time as Barnsley just avoided relegation to the Second Division and Anderson departed to become assistant manager at Middlesbrough under Bryan Robson.

John McGovern

Clough's 'little lamb', as wherever Cloughie went, "Border" was sure to follow and did so from Hartlepools to Derby, then Leeds and finally to Forest. McGovern was surprisingly released in 1982 to take over at Bolton. He tasted little success at Burnden Park, and also had forgettable stints at Rotherham and Woking.

Frank Clark

Clough nominated the former Newcastle and Forest left-back as his eventual successor, and indeed that is just what happened, Clark succeeding Clough and guiding Forest back into the top flight and Europe before quitting in 1996. Clark's time at Forest was sandwiched by spells at Leyton Orient and Manchester City. To this day, he remains Forest's most successful post-Clough manager.

Peter Withe

The ex-Forest and Aston Villa target-man had one of the most disastrous spells as a top flight boss when he managed Wimbledon for 105 days in 1991/92, winning just one game out of 13. He had a more winning time in charge of the national squads of Thailand and then Indonesia.

Larry Lloyd

The defensive stalwart's Forest career came to an end in March 1981 when he was allowed to take over at Wigan Athletic. He led them to promotion after a year then took over at Notts County, then in the First Division, who he led briefly to the league's top spot before they plummeted into the relegation zone in 1983/84, and Lloyd was sacked.

Peter Shilton

Forest's greatest ever keeper had an up-and-down two year spell in charge of Plymouth Argyle, commencing February 1992. Argyle were relegated to the third tier in 1992/93 then lost in the play-offs the following term. Shilton quit with a second relegation looking likely.

Archie Gemmill

The energetic midfield man was signed twice by Clough, once for Derby and once for Forest, and also had two spells as a coach at Forest between 1984 and 1994. Touted as a potential future Forest boss, Gemmill instead had an unremarkable two-season spell at Rotherham, before joining Scotland's coaching staff.

Gary Mills

Mills became a hugely successful non-league manager, with Grantham, King's Lynn, Tamworth (twice), Alfreton and York City. His one spell in league management was not a success, as his ten months at the helm of Notts County in 2004 saw them relegated to the league's bottom tier. Mills got York back into the league in 2012.

Trevor Francis

The country's first £1m man surprisingly became a controversial manager during spells at QPR, Sheffield Wednesday, Birmingham and Crystal Palace. He famously tried to ban QPR midfielder Martin Allen from attending the birth of his first child, and missed out on the opportunity to sign Eric Cantona for the Owls.

Frank Gray

Signed in 1979 to replace Frank Clark at left-back, Gray also played very briefly under Clough at Leeds. He managed Darlington for a year in 1991/92, later managing in non-league with Farnborough, Grays Athletic, Woking and Basingstoke.

Stuart Gray

The former Forest man had one of the briefest spells as a Premier League boss in 2001 when he lasted three months at Southampton. He went on to have an unsuccessful spell in charge at Northampton.

Jürgen Röber

The talented midfielder lasted only briefly at Forest as his wife wanted to return to their native Germany. He then became a successful manager, taking charge at Rot-Weiss Essen, Stuttgart, Hertha Berlin, Wolfsburg, Partizan Belgrade, Borussia Dortmund, Saturn Ramenskow and Akarapor.

Steve Wigley

Another blink-and-you-missed-him Premier League manager, the former Reds winger managed just one win in 14 while in charge at Southampton. He also had a brief spell as caretaker at Bolton.

Colin Todd

Todd had three spells under Clough, with Sunderland, Derby and Forest. The defender had a varied managerial career over two decades, with spells at Middlesbrough, Bolton, Swindon, Derby, Bradford and Darlington.

Danny Wilson

The midfielder was one Clough maybe should have stuck with, but was sold to Brighton after just ten games. Wilson became a successful lower-division manager, taking charge at Barnsley, Sheffield Wednesday, Bristol City, MK Dons, Hartlepool, Swindon and Sheffield United.

Paul Hart

The former Reds centre-back was promoted from Academy boss at Forest to replace David Platt in July 2001 and took Forest to the 2002/03 play-offs before being sacked in February 2004. He also has had terms in charge at Chesterfield, Barnsley, Rushden & Diamonds, Portsmouth, QPR, Crystal Palace and Swindon.

Kenny Swain

Full-back Swain had a season as boss of Wigan and was a caretaker at Grimsby before taking charge of the England under-16 squad in 2004.

Nigel Clough

The "number nine" famously followed in his father's footsteps by taking charge of Derby County in January 2009. This came after a successful ten-year spell in the hot-seat at Burton Albion, guiding them to the brink of league football.

Stuart Pearce

The club legend failed to save Forest from relegation in 1996/97 as caretaker boss following Frank Clark's resignation and left the club at the end of the season. He managed Manchester City between 2005 and 2007 and then took charge of the England under-21 side.

Brian Laws

Another ex-Red, like Wilson and Hart, who went on to be a success in the lower divisions. He managed Grimsby, Scunthorpe and Sheffield Wednesday before leading Burnley in the Premier League in 2009/10, seeing them relegated at the end of the season.

Roy Keane

The controversial yet exquisitely talented midfielder took charge at Sunderland between 2006 and 2008 and guided them back into the Premier League, then had a less successful two-year stint at Ipswich.

OLD MAN RILEY

When Forest reported back for pre-season training for the 1987/88 season, Brian Clough's plans to reinvent the club based on young players seemed complete. With the free transfers to veterans Garry Birtles and Ian Bowyer, and the defection of Johnny Metgod to Tottenham, the oldest player now on Forest's staff was the reserve team striker David Riley, at the ripe old age of 26. Forest's first side that season was as follows, with the player's age in brackets: Steve Sutton (26), Gary Fleming (20), Stuart Pearce (25), Des Walker (21), Colin Foster (23), David Campbell (22), Franz Carr (20), Neil Webb (24), Nigel Clough (21), Paul Wilkinson (22), Lee Glover (17). Riley was sold to Port Vale in October 1987 after making just 12 appearances in four years at Forest.

THE TRICKY TREE

While club badges can change as often as kits, the Forest emblem dates back almost 40 years and was first worn at the start of the 1973/74 season. It was created by David Lewis, a designer and lecturer in graphic design at Trent Polytechnic, with the tree representing Forest, and three wavy lines standing for the club's proximity to the River Trent. Lewis' design was selected via a competition, and – allegedly – beat into second place one designed by a Derby County fan whose effort was encircled by a series of dots and dashes that spelled out "Derby will forever rule supreme" in Morse code. The previous badge, which had been adopted in 1957, had been Nottingham's coat of arms with the castle on top of the shield replaced by the initials NFFC and was replaced as Forest could not obtain copyright. Prior to that, Forest had worn a circular badge containing the slightly evil-looking Jolly Forester character with the NFFC initials beneath.

ROY KEANE: A GREAT PLAYER AND ONE OF THE MANY WHO PLAYED UNDER BRIAN CLOUGH AND LATER WENT INTO MANAGEMENT

NUMBER TWO IS...

Viv Anderson. The Clifton-born youngster became the first black player to sign for Forest, and is regarded as the first black player to play for the full England football team (although it is acknowledged now that Leeds United's Paul Reaney could also claim such a title). A long-striding right-back, "Spider" made his debut for Forest in 1974 but didn't gain a regular place in the club's number two shirt until 1976 after Liam O'Kane's retirement through injury. Anderson came through the usual racist taunts that blighted football in the 1970s (he complained once to Brian Clough during a game that an unnamed opposition player was calling him a "black b*****d", to which Clough advised "well go back out there and call him a "white b*****d") to emerge as England's best right-back and easily the best right-back ever to play for Forest. He would have (and should have) won more England caps than the 30 he did acquire if not for the favouritism at the time shown to Liverpool players which meant Phil Neal was regularly selected ahead of him. Anderson's speed and clean tackling remained a feature of Forest's play until 1984, by which time the championship-winning side had completed dissipated and Anderson joined Arsenal. He later served Manchester United, Sheffield Wednesday, Barnsley (where he had a spell as player-manager) and Middlesbrough. Anderson was awarded an MBE in January 2000, and later worked as a goodwill ambassador for the Football Association.

A TASTY COMBINATION

In March 1990 Forest surprisingly signed Darlington's prolific (in the Fourth Division, anyhow) David Currie. Despite a decent and goal-scoring debut, it was soon clear that the three-division step up for Currie was too far, and he only managed four appearances for Forest (and another four as a substitute). He did give rise to a culinary oddity though – with Scottish midfielder Brian Rice already at the club, Brian Clough was able to name Currie and Rice as his subs' bench for a couple of games.

PALINDROMIC PLAYERS

Just to possibly confuse opposition players or referees (or maybe because they were decent players), for three years in the 1970s Forest had both Neil Martin and Martin O'Neill as first-team regulars.

GO USA

Forest's first ever trip to the States occurred in May and June 1965 when a party of players and officials journeyed over the Atlantic to tour the US and Canada for a month. The side played 11 games, losing only two – oddly both to non-North American teams, these being the German outfit Hanover 96 and Hibernian from Scotland, both of whom were touring the country at the same time. Forest's best victory came in their opener against Hartford South Carolina, who they hammered 8-2 with Ian Storey-Moore scoring four goals and Chris Crowe adding three.

NEVER GO BACK

Prior to the 1960s, it was almost unheard of for a player to leave a club and then return for a second stint with the same side at a future date. It wasn't until 1981 that a player came back to the City Ground after leaving, stalwart Ian Bowyer who was rescued by Brian Clough from an unhappy year at Sunderland. Since then, those who've come back for a second bite at the red-shirted cherry are Garry Birtles, Gary Mills, John Robertson, Calvin Plummer, Steve Hodge, Neil Webb, Des Walker, Alan Rogers, Jon Olav Hjelde, Jack Lester, Andy Reid and Marlon Harewood.

WER HAT DIE HOSEN AN?

German midfielder Jürgen Röber was one of the few bright sparks of Forest's dismal 1981/82 campaign (it was one of only two times the side finished outside the top half of the top flight under Brian Clough since their promotion in 1977), serving hints he might finally answer the problem of the missing midfield engine since the sale of Archie Gemmill. However, Mrs Röber had other ideas and as her fondness for England hadn't grown above 'tolerate' her and her husband returned instead to the fatherland, and Jürgen signed a contract with Bayer Leverkusen.

SNOOKERING YOU TONIGHT

An exhibition of snooker was given in March 1974 by one of the game's then top players, John Spencer, at Forest's social club, during which he made a record break of 113. Sadly, there is very little evidence to suggest whether or not this feat has ever been bettered.

100 GOALS – AND RELEGATED

Forest didn't have much to celebrate at the end of a very tepid 1981/82, but at least they could take some pride at the performance of their reserve side who finished fourth in the Central League, scoring 102 goals and conceding just 37. The stiffs' reward for such a decent season was, bizarrely, relegation. The Central League was restructured at the end of 1981/82, with ten new teams entering. This led to an unwieldy league of 32 sides so the decision was made to split it into a two-tier system of two 16-team divisions. This led to the question of which six teams should be 'demoted', so instead of the bottom six teams from the previous term being so sent down, lots were drawn instead, and Forest were one of the unlucky six.

TRANSFER FLOPS #1

In the summer of 1969 Forest manager Matt Gillies committed one of his frequent sins against the club in selling Joe Baker to Sunderland. The season began with no replacement ready, so it was a case of filling in the gaps. Youngsters Colin Hall and Graham Collier proved too raw, while the experienced but versatile Dave Hilley couldn't find the net often enough. Entering the transfer market, Gillies' first choice to replace Baker was the Rangers striker and future Manchester United manager Alex Ferguson, but when Ferguson's wife declared she was not keen to move to England Gillies signed a different Alex, Ayr United's Alex 'Dixie' Ingram, for £45,000 in January 1970. Things began well for the Scot as he scored in his second game, against Sunderland, but he ended the season with only three goals in 16 league matches. The 1970/71 season was even worse – Ingram never looked anything like a fearsome goal-getter and after a further 12 games (and zero goals) he was dropped from the side, never to return. Forest signed another Scot, veteran Neil Martin, to replace Alex but he hardly fared better, initially at least, scoring once in 12 games. Ingram returned to Ayr in February 1971 and recovered his previous prowess, and indeed in the 1973/74 season formed a strike partnership with the aforementioned Ferguson. He returned to the City Ground in 1976 for an Anglo-Scottish Cup match, and at the time of writing, is the vice-chairman at Somerton Park.

IN THE WRONG END?

There was perhaps nothing noteworthy about the goal Ian Wallace scored for Forest against Southampton on 13th November 1982 except perhaps the goalkeeper who conceded it. The man in question was Peter Shilton, and it was the first goal a Forest player had scored against the former Reds legend after he had left the City Ground the previous summer.

JIMMY GRIEVES

In 1982 marksman-turned-pundit Jimmy Greaves confidently predicted that Brian Clough would struggle to manage Nottingham Forest without his right-hand man Peter Taylor, and said that he would pay £100 to charity if Forest were not in the bottom six of the First Division at Christmas. At it turned out, the former Chelsea and Spurs sharp-shooter could hardly have been more wrong, as at the end of the Christmas programme Forest sat proudly in second position, six points behind leaders Liverpool.

THRASHED?

On 19th January 1983 Forest were rudely dumped out of the League Cup at the quarter-final stage by Manchester United, losing 4-0. This defeat informed all just how consistently Forest had performed for over a decade, as it was their first loss by such a heavy margin since 27th March 1972 when Leeds United had slaughtered the relegation-bound Reds 6-1. It was therefore also the worst defeat at the time suffered by the Reds under the stewardship of Brian Clough.

THE LONGEST GOAL?

On 27th December 1971, with the usual Boxing Day games instead taking place 24 hours later, Ian Storey-Moore scored a legendary goal against the much-fancied Arsenal that is probably one of the best ever solo goals scored by a Forest player. Picking up the ball from a defensive header by Tommy Gemmell, Moore managed to run virtually the full length of the pitch, 74 and a half yards in total, twisting and turning and beating Gunner after Gunner, before planting his shot firmly past Bob Wilson. Television cameras were on hand to record Alan Ball's debut for Arsenal, but viewers were treated to something far, far grander.

NEVER LOOKED BACK

Those of a certain vintage will remember David Frost, who leapt to fame in the early 1960s as host of the ground-breaking satirical TV programme *That Was The Week That Was*, and who since has enjoyed a continuing career in the broadcast media. Frost was a keen amateur footballer in his latter schooldays and, upon a successful trial, was actually offered professional terms as a goalkeeper by Nottingham Forest in the late-1950s, but rejected them in order to pursue his academic career. By coincidence, Frost was portrayed by Michael Sheen in the film *Frost/Nixon*, the same actor who later played Brian Clough in *The Damned United*. Sprinting forwards nearly half a century, the actor Matt Smith, best known for portraying the 11th incarnation of the Doctor in *Doctor Who*, was a successful youth footballer with Forest, as well as Northampton Town and Leicester City. A serious back injury put paid to Smith's footballing ambitions and he instead turned to acting and ended up traversing the known Universe.

OH BROTHER

Whereas there have been a few pairs of brothers who have played for Forest, only one set of three siblings have played for the club: Andy, Kevin and Michael Dawson, although they never played in the same side together. All three were born in Northallerton in North Yorkshire – Andy on 20th October 1978, Kevin on 18th June 1981 and Michael on 18th November 1983. Left-back Andy made only one appearance for the Reds before moving on to Scunthorpe United and then Hull City, with whom he played in every division including the Premiership. Kevin was a centre-back who appeared 11 times for Forest before being sold to Chesterfield in 2002, and later drifted into non-league football. Michael, also a central defender, broke into the Forest first team in 2002 and soon formed an excellent partnership with veteran Des Walker. Michael was a solid but fair defender who had excellent distribution skills for a centre-back, and it was clear he was destined for bigger things than Forest could at the time provide. He signed for Tottenham on deadline day, 2005 for a combined fee with Andy Reid of £8m. His career moved on at White Hart Lane and he eventually made the England squad, journeying to the 2010 World Cup as a replacement for the injured Rio Ferdinand.

FOREST v THE REST

Opponents	P	W	D	L	F	A	W%	Av
Accrington	2	1	0	1	4	1	0.500	1.50
Aldershot	4	2	2	0	11	2	0.500	2.00
Arsenal	92	25	22	45	102	141	0.272	1.05
Aston Villa	108	31	27	50	152	186	0.287	1.11
Barnsley	71	25	20	26	101	98	0.352	1.34
Birmingham	88	34	24	30	116	124	0.386	1.43
Blackburn R	96	29	24	43	130	177	0.302	1.16
Blackpool	76	29	23	24	107	93	0.382	1.45
Bolton W	70	23	18	29	96	107	0.329	1.24
Bournemouth	10	4	3	3	13	10	0.400	1.50
Bradford PA	36	17	6	13	64	60	0.472	1.58
Bradford C	40	19	12	9	60	42	0.475	1.73
Brentford	18	6	7	5	26	20	0.333	1.39
Brighton	24	11	6	7	33	20	0.458	1.63
Bristol C	68	29	25	14	104	70	0.426	1.65
Bristol R	20	9	5	6	35	28	0.450	1.60
Burnley	94	34	24	36	138	139	0.362	1.34
Burton U	2	2	0	0	4	0	1.000	3.00
Bury	84	26	21	37	126	135	0.310	1.18
Cardiff C	42	12	10	20	46	61	0.286	1.10
Carlisle U	12	6	3	3	20	9	0.500	1.75
Charlton A	32	11	10	11	43	47	0.344	1.34
Chelsea	84	25	26	33	121	107	0.298	1.20
Cheltenham	4	4	0	0	11	1	1.000	3.00
Chesterfield	22	8	5	9	33	32	0.364	1.32
Colchester U	4	2	1	1	4	3	0.500	1.75
Coventry C	86	43	27	16	137	85	0.500	1.81
Crewe A	16	9	5	2	29	12	0.563	2.00
Crystal P	48	23	12	13	75	48	0.479	1.69
Darlington	4	2	1	1	9	5	0.500	1.75
Darwen	2	2	0	0	8	1	1.000	3.00
Derby Co	80	33	19	28	128	123	0.413	1.48
Doncaster R	32	15	9	8	55	31	0.469	1.69
Everton	120	42	26	52	147	198	0.350	1.27
Exeter C	4	2	2	0	12	2	0.500	2.00
Fulham	82	25	52	5	107	122	0.305	1.55
Gainsborough	4	4	0	0	10	4	1.000	3.00

Opponents	P	W	D	L	F	A	W%	Av
Gillingham	18	9	9	0	41	23	0.500	2.00
Glossop	12	5	1	6	17	16	0.417	1.33
Grimsby T	40	17	11	12	63	52	0.425	1.55
Hartlepool U	4	3	0	1	7	4	0.750	2.25
Hereford U	2	2	0	0	5	3	1.000	3.00
Huddersfield	38	11	11	16	44	51	0.289	1.16
Hull City	56	26	8	22	82	64	0.464	1.54
Ipswich T	60	30	13	17	88	66	0.500	1.72
Leeds C	10	5	0	5	16	22	0.500	1.50
Leeds U	78	22	29	27	91	111	0.282	1.22
Leicester C	94	35	22	37	147	137	0.376	1.35
Leyton O	46	23	14	9	74	44	0.500	1.80
Lincoln C	26	12	9	5	52	35	0.462	1.73
Liverpool	100	26	24	50	99	167	0.260	1.02
Luton T	56	22	14	20	85	82	0.393	1.43
Manchester C	90	27	26	37	124	139	0.300	1.19
Manchester U	96	29	23	44	128	176	0.302	1.15
Middlesbrough	66	21	27	18	93	90	0.318	1.36
Millwall	52	17	17	18	74	77	0.327	1.31
MK Dons	2	1	0	1	3	1	0.500	1.50
Newcastle U	89	27	20	42	101	136	0.303	1.13
Newport Co	7	6	0	1	21	9	0.857	2.57
Northampton	10	3	6	1	14	12	0.300	1.50
Norwich C	62	24	16	22	92	80	0.387	1.42
Notts County	86	35	23	28	120	107	0.407	1.49
Oldham A	42	17	8	17	70	71	0.405	1.40
Oxford U	18	8	4	6	25	18	0.444	1.56
Peterborough U	6	5	0	1	9	4	0.833	2.50
Plymouth A	44	20	6	18	67	62	0.455	1.50
Port Vale	48	25	10	13	89	61	0.521	1.77
Portsmouth	34	17	4	13	48	34	0.500	1.62
Preston NE	86	27	22	37	126	135	0.314	1.20
QPR	50	20	17	13	73	53	0.400	1.54
Reading	30	13	7	10	45	36	0.433	1.53
Rotherham C	6	4	1	1	12	4	0.667	2.17
Rotherham U	24	11	8	5	45	36	0.458	1.71
Scunthorpe U	8	2	2	4	11	13	0.250	1.00
Sheffield U	100	40	26	34	148	125	0.400	1.46
Sheffield W	118	47	23	48	163	161	0.398	1.39

Opponents	P	W	D	L	F	A	W%	Av
South Shields	12	6	3	3	26	19	0.500	1.75
Southampton	98	42	21	35	151	144	0.429	1.50
Southend U	10	5	2	3	19	11	0.500	1.70
Stockport Co	26	9	9	8	33	32	0.346	1.38
Stoke C	98	41	28	29	146	119	0.418	1.54
Sunderland	86	28	22	36	109	134	0.326	1.23
Swansea C	58	24	13	21	96	85	0.414	1.47
Swindon T	16	9	5	2	32	12	0.563	2.00
Torquay U	4	1	0	3	6	8	0.250	0.75
Tottenham H	104	31	24	49	138	175	0.298	1.13
Tranmere R	16	7	8	1	22	15	0.438	1.81
Walsall	16	6	4	6	28	23	0.375	1.38
Watford	36	13	13	10	45	41	0.361	1.44
West Brom	114	40	23	51	172	197	0.351	1.25
West Ham U	104	38	25	41	151	156	0.365	1.34
Wigan A	4	1	3	0	5	4	0.250	1.50
Wimbledon	30	11	6	13	44	39	0.367	1.30
Wolves	114	37	24	53	167	198	0.325	1.18
Yeovil T	6	5	0	1	10	6	0.833	2.50
York C	4	2	1	1	6	5	0.500	1.75

W% - percentage of games won out of all games played

Av – average points gained per games (based on 3pts for a win)

SORRY WE'RE LATE

As you might imagine, wartime football was a pretty haphazard affair as the country's resources were stretched to shattering point. In February 1918 Forest travelled via train to Leeds to fulfil a fixture but due to cancellations and delays, turned up with only seven players. Leeds City leant Forest their left-winger Billy Hampson so that the visitors had at least a chance of equality, and after ten minutes three of the missing players, goalkeeper Josh Johnson (Fred Banks had had to start the match in goal), Harry Wightman and Harry Poole, arrived at the ground. Forest lost the game 2-0, with Wightman scoring an own goal.

OFF ON HIS TODD

Colin Todd had one of the most memorable home debuts for Forest, after signing from Birmingham City in the summer of 1992. He was sent off after 70 minutes for handball.

FOREST'S PLAYER OF THE SEASON AWARD

1976/77	Tony Woodcock
1977/78	Kenny Burns
1978/79	Garry Birtles
1979/80	Larry Lloyd
1980/81	Kenny Burns
1981/82	Peter Shilton
1982/83	Steve Hodge
1983/84	Chris Fairclough
1984/85	Jim McInally
1985/86	Nigel Clough
1986/87	Des Walker
1987/88	Nigel Clough
1988/89	Stuart Pearce
1989/90	Des Walker
1990/91	Stuart Pearce
1991/92	Des Walker
1992/93	Steve Sutton
1993/94	David Phillips
1994/95	Steve Stone
1995/96	Stuart Pearce
1996/97	Colin Cooper
1997/98	Pierre van Hooijdonk
1998/99	Alan Rogers
1999/00	Dave Beasant
2000/01	Chris Bart-Williams
2001/02	Gareth Williams
2002/03	David Johnson
2003/04	Andy Reid
2004/05	Paul Gerrard
2005/06	Ian Breckin
2006/07	Grant Holt
2007/08	Julian Bennett
2008/09	Chris Cohen
2009/10	Lee Camp
2010/11	Luke Chambers
2011/12	Garath McCleary

PLATTITUDE

While most Forest supporters, if not all, will not remember David Platt's tenure in the hot-seat with a happy smile, Platt did succeed in writing his name into Forest folklore on two occasions. Platt is the only Forest manager to have scored for the club while in charge, and is the only manager to have been sent off too. Platt's dismissal came on 16th October 1999, late in a second tier game against Sheffield United. It was the first and only red card of Platt's career, and it was for a professional foul on Paul Devlin. Forest were already down to ten men at the time as Nigel Quashie had been sent off in the first half and ended up on the wrong end of a 2-1 result. Platt's only goal for Forest came on 28th August 2000 in an incident-packed game against Crystal Palace at Selhurst Park. Platt had scored the second as Forest took a 3-0 lead, only for the home team to pull it back to 3-2 with eight minutes to go. A minute later Fan Zhiyi was brought down on the edge of the penalty area by Dave Beasant, and referee Oliver both sent the Reds' keeper off and awarded Palace a spot-kick sparking ridiculous scenes as the Forest and Palace players started throwing their handbags at each other. Substitute goalkeeper Barry Roche came on for Jack Lester, but was left floundering as Julian Gray successfully converted to make it 3-3 – or so it seemed. Oliver decided he hadn't had enough fun for the afternoon and ordered the kick to be retaken, allegedly for encroachment. Gray stepped up again and with his first touch in league football, Roche made the save to end the game and ensure Forest gained all three points.

YOU'RE IN...YOU'RE OUT

In February 1993 Brian Clough surprised fans in announcing the usual deputy for the injured Stuart Pearce, Brett Williams, would not be selected for the forthcoming game at Middlesbrough, with 17-year-old Craig Armstrong being handed a start. There came naturally a deal of fuss over a new young gun, and Armstrong was interviewed by the local news and TV, probed as to how it felt to be so raw yet expected to fill Psycho's boots. Come the game and Armstrong proudly trotted out...to sit on the bench as centre-back Steve Chettle took the number three shirt. Armstrong had to wait until March 1996 to finally make his bow.

LAST MAN STANDING (1959)

Very sadly, only one of Forest's 1959 FA Cup winning side remains alive at the time of writing, wing-half "Gentleman" Jeff Whitefoot, who was also known as "Sugar" to his colleagues after a popular TV programme of the time, *Sugarfoot*. Along with Bob McKinlay and Jack Burkitt, Jeff formed one of the club's most memorable half-back lines that helped Forest beat Luton in the club's first FA Cup Final for over 60 years. Jeff had served Manchester United for seven years before turning down a move to Forest in 1957, joining Grimsby Town instead. He finally moved to the City Ground in July 1958 for £11,500 and played for the Reds until retiring in 1968. He went into the typical footballer's trade of publican, becoming host at the Three Horse Shoes at East Leake.

BOXING DAY BLAST

On Boxing Day 1924, a relegation-haunted Forest were a goal and a man down to FA Cup holders Bolton Wanderers, influential outside-left Harry Martin having been taken off injured early in the game – and there were no substitutes in the 1920s. With 15 minutes to go, Forest were awarded a penalty and, as Martin was the usual taker, skipper Bob Wallace asked for a volunteer. When not one player declared himself man enough, outside-right Syd Gibson raced into the dressing room and, along with the trainer, carried the injured Martin out on to the pitch and propped him up along with the ball on the penalty spot. An expectant hush fell over the City Ground as Martin swung his left boot at the ball. He connected with such velocity that the ball blasted past England goalkeeper Dick Pym and into the goal to secure Forest a precious point. Martin collapsed and was carried back to the dressing room with cheers in his ears.

THE FIRST COMPETITIVE GOAL

Nottingham Forest Football Club first entered the Association Challenge Cup in 1878, and were drawn at home to Notts County. The match took place at the Beeston Cricket Ground and Forest triumphed 3-1. The scorer of Forest's first goal was JP Turner (who is thought to have had the first name of John but there are no records of the time to prove this) and as such is regarded as the scorer of Forest's first ever competitive goal, on 16th November 1878.

UNLUCKY LIAM

Defender Liam O'Kane was never the luckiest with injuries, suffering a broken leg in his early 20s and further woes that finished his career in 1977 despite him still being only 28. After signing for the Reds from Derry City in November 1968, Liam played over 200 games for the club, and scored one goal – but one that didn't count. Infamously, the 1973/74 FA Cup quarter-final between Forest and Newcastle was declared void after United had won 4-3 despite being 3-1 down and a man down, the red-carded Pat Howard, following a ten-minute pitch invasion by the Newcastle fans that had somewhat influenced the outcome of the game. O'Kane had been the scorer of Forest's second goal, a shot from outside the area after a goalmouth scramble, but of course said strike was chalked off. O'Kane went on to serve as a member of Forest's backroom staff once he'd retired, staying at the club until 2005.

TIME OFF FOR A CUP FINAL? NO CHANCE!

Of course if your side reaches the final of a major cup competition and it unfortunately clashes with work, a well-meaning boss may acquiesce and allow you the time off to support your beloved team. But how about if you're playing in the final? Such a disaster almost befell Forest's outside-left Alf Spouncer prior to the 1898 FA Cup Final at Crystal Palace against Derby County. Spouncer was unable to get the time off work to train with his colleagues prior to the match, so instead was forced to 'prepare himself quietly at home under the care of a qualified man.'

UNCLE BILLY

While Bob McKinlay's contribution to Forest's history is monumental, as the club's record appearance maker, the previous contribution of his uncle Billy shouldn't be overlooked. Like his nephew, Billy was born in Lochgelly, in Fife, and was described as "an ideal right-half in every sense of the word with excellent ball control, a rare turn of speed and, not infrequently, a sixth forward". Billy played over 350 games for the Reds and once retired, became Forest's chief scout in Scotland. Among his recommendations was, of course, his nephew, Bobby. Billy passed away in 1976.

HAPPY BIRTHDAY NIGEL

There was an interesting note in the match programme for the game at the City Ground against Sunderland on 17th March 1976, congratulating Brian Clough's youngest son, Nigel, on becoming ten years old on the 19th. Of course the writer would not have known that the name of Nigel Clough would feature regularly in Forest's programmes from 1983 onwards.

NO EASY GAMES? PERHAPS IN 1964 ...?

There are no easy games in international football these days, or so they say. Things must have been considerably different back in the 1960s then, when the New Zealand national team came to the City Ground on 20th April 1964 for a game against Forest's first team and were hammered 8-0. Forest's goals were scored by Frank Wignall with a hat-trick, Colin Addison and Alan Hinton with two each, and a further effort from Ian Storey-Moore.

FORTRESS CITY GROUND

On 5th April 2010, Forest drew 0-0 with Cardiff City at the City Ground, hence ending a club record sequence of 12 consecutive home league victories. The club's 100% home record in that period had begun with a 4-1 defeat of Doncaster Rovers on 28th November 2009. There then followed victories over Leicester City (5-0), Preston (3-0), Coventry (2-0), Reading (2-1), QPR (5-0), Sheffield Wednesday (2-1), Sheffield United (1-0), Middlesbrough (1-0 – equalling the then club record), Swansea City (1-0 – setting a new club record), Peterborough United (1-0) and finally Crystal Palace (2-0). The then manager Billy Davies therefore achieved something that Brian Clough failed to do in all of his years at the City Ground.

RINGWHO?

Probably the most obscure goalscorer in Forest's history is one T Ringberg, who was on target in the 88th minute of Forest's tour match in Sweden in the summer of 1986 against Aelmhult IF. Forest won 8-0, with Neil Webb enjoying an outing as a striker and registering six goals to his name. Apparently, T Ringberg was the tour courier, who played the final ten minutes of the game as a substitute for Ian Bowyer.

A GRAND GESTURE

The first league game at Old Trafford after February 1958's air disaster in Munich which devastated Manchester United's first team was a 1-1 draw against Nottingham Forest. The effect the air crash had on the United team can be emphasised by comparing the line-up of that game with that of the previous home fixture against Arsenal, which was: Gregg, Foulkes, Byrne*, Colman*, M Jones*, Edwards*, Morgans, Charlton, T Taylor*, Viollet, Scanlon. Against Forest the side was: Gregg, Foulkes, Greaves, Goodwin, Cope, Crowther, Webster, E Taylor, Dawson, Pearson, Brennan. Players asterisked either died in the crash or later from their injuries. Stewart Imlach scored for Forest and Alex Dawson for United. Forest, alongside Liverpool, were one of only two teams who offered to loan United players so they were able to fulfil their fixture commitments.

BRIEFLY EXCELLENT

Perhaps the most unexpected name to appear on the list of the winners of Forest's Player of the Season award is Jim McInally, who won it for 1984/85 despite only playing 24 league games that season. Signed from Celtic in the summer of 1984, right-back McInally had to force his way into the team past Bryn Gunn and Gary Mills (usually a midfielder) and emerged as a genuine replacement for Viv Anderson. The Forest support rewarded him at the end of the term with the title. Unfortunately, a few games into the 1985/86 season McInally was injured, and found his way back barred by Gary Fleming. He was sold in the summer of 1986 having only played 36 games for Forest. After a brief spell with Coventry he returned north of the border to Dundee United.

A PERFECT TEN

While Forest have only ever entered double figures in goals scored in a single match in official competition twice, they have reached that target frequently in friendlies. In 1976 Forest beat the Spanish team Serverence 10-0 with Barry Butlin (four) and Ian Bowyer (three) leading the goals charge. However, Forest were less than respectful to the Spaniards when they took off Bowyer towards the end of the game, and replaced him with the substitute goalkeeper John Middleton, who played up front. The move seemed justified though when Middleton scored Forest's tenth and final goal.

HOT SHOTS!

Forest's most lethal marksmen. League games and full appearances only, minimum 50 games to qualify.

1   Wally Ardron (123 goals in 183 games)...............................0.672
2   Stan Collymore (41 goals in 64 games)..............................0.641
3   Jim Barrett (64 goals in 105 games) 0.610
4   Johnny Dent (117 goals in 197 games) 0.594
5   Enoch West (94 goals in 170 games) 0.553
6   Pierre van Hooijdonk (36 goals in 68 games) 0.539
7   Tom Peacock (57 goals in 109 games) 0.523
8   Dave "Boy" Martin (41 goals in 81 games) 0.506
9   Billy Dickinson (68 goals in 137 games).............................0.496
10 Grenville Morris (199 goals in 420 games).........................0.478

At the other end of the scale, of those players who scored for Forest in their careers, the most goal-shy player is Geoff Thomas (the 1950s/60s version) who scored once in 405 league games.

SAFE HANDS

Forest's most reliable goalkeepers. League games and full appearances only, minimum 50 games to qualify. The figure at the right-hand side of this table is the average goals conceded per game.

1   Peter Shilton (176 goals in 203 games)...............................0.867
2   Paul Smith (116 goals in 120 games) 0.967
3   John Middleton (90 goals in 90 games) 1.000
4   Lee Camp (169 goals in 152 games)....................................1.112
5   Hans van Breukelen (68 goals in 61 games)........................1.115
6   Steve Sutton (227 goals in 199 games) 1.141
7   Darren Ward (141 goals in 123 games)...............................1.146
8   Dave Beasant (174 goals in 139 games) 1.252
9   Paul Gerrard (89 goals in 71 games) 1.254
10 Harry Walker (374 goals in 293 games)..............................1.276

Forest's most leaky stoppers are T Tebbutt (one game), John Wagstaff (one game) and Mick Harby (three games), each with an average concede of five goals per match played.

DRUNK LEICESTER

Forest's record league win was a rather stonking 12-0 victory against Leicester Fosse (now of course, City) on 21st April 1909. Leicester were already relegated from the top flight by then, but as Forest were in a huge clump of clubs fighting to stave off relegation at the time, several other teams cried 'foul' and the Football League naturally ordered an enquiry, which was held at the Grand Hotel in Leicester. The hapless Leicester players were quick to confess – the reason they had all played so badly (in the game, Alf Spouncer, Billy Hooper and "Knocker" West had all claimed hat-tricks and the score had been kept down to a dozen thanks to the heroics of Fosse's goalkeeper Horace Bailey) was because they'd all been mightily hung-over. A former team-mate, Bob Turner (now at Everton), had returned to Leicester the previous day to celebrate his recent wedding with his ex-colleagues. The celebrations had continued into the early hours with the Fosse personnel completely forgetting they had a match to play later that day. The Football League decided that they had little option but for the result to stand, much to the annoyance of Manchester City who were relegated along with bottom-of-the-table Leicester. Such was the closeness of the competition that year, the relegated Manchester City side, who finished 19th, were only four points behind Woolwich Arsenal, who finished sixth. A sobered-up Leicester team took on Turner's new Everton charges a few days after the Forest match and lost 4-2.

TAKE ME OUT TO THE BALL GAME

Forest were champions of England for the first time in 1900, as some knowledgeable Reds fans will tell you. You will then of course correct them, as Forest's first league title was won in 1978, but you would be wrong. In 1900 Nottingham Forest FC were indeed the champions of England, but at baseball. Several of the Forest side at the time (including football goalkeeper and baseball captain Dan Allsopp) played both football and baseball, which remained popular in England until the start of the Second World War, professionally. Forest beat Derby County Baseball Club (who of course played at the Baseball Ground, sharing it at the time with Derby County Football Club) 17-16 in the final. This was revenge for the defeat by Derby in the previous season's final by the more one-sided score of 14-3.

KNOCKER NICKED

After the days of Sandy Higgins and Grenville Morris and before Tom Peacock and Wally Ardron, the most prolific marksman to wear the garibaldi was Enoch "Knocker" West. Despite being a Notts lad, born in Hucknall Tonkard, West joined Forest in 1905 from Sheffield United for a princely £5 fee. He formed an impressive partnership with Morris, but his 14 goals (and Morris' 19) were not enough to keep Forest in the top flight, and they were relegated for the first time. The following season West scored 14 again as Forest bounced back at the first attempt but a year later West romped away in the scoring tables with 28 in 35 games, then followed this up with 22 in 34 the following season. After 1909/10 West was transferred to Manchester United and helped them to the league title in 1911. His prolific career continued, scoring 80 goals in 181 games for the Red Devils. Things took the worst turn imaginable for West in 1915 when he and six other players were found guilty of fixing the game between Manchester United and Liverpool on 2nd April 1915. It was discovered that a large amount of money had been placed at odds of 7/1 on a 2-0 United win, the score with which the game finished. All players were found guilty, including West who vehemently protested his innocence, going so far as to sue the FA for libel. West's case failed, and his ban stood. After the First World War all players involved in the scandal had their bans lifted in recognition of them serving their country during hostilities – except for West, who still refused to admit his guilt. West never played professional football again. His ban was finally lifted, in 1945, by which time he was 59. "Knocker" West died in 1965.

THE NAME GAME

The most appropriately named player to play for Forest must be John Forrest, who played a few games on the wing for the club in the early-1930s. On the other side of the coin, in more recent times, turning out have been Jack Lester and Matt Derbyshire, neither of whom were blessed with Forest-friendly monikers, although in the case of the former the popular penalty-winning striker managed to generate the chant "there's only one decent Lester" from the crowd.

NUMBER THREE IS...

Stuart Pearce, who else? Easily the best left-back ever to pull on the garibaldi red shirt of Nottingham Forest, "Psycho" patrolled the left at the City Ground (and many other grounds) for 12 years. Pearce could tackle with firm ferocity, shoot with unbelievable venom, race into opposition penalty boxes to become an extra forward and was also a set-piece expert. Pearce was virtually unheard of when picked up from Coventry City along with his team-mate Ian Butterworth in the summer of 1985, having had two seasons at Highfield Road following a step up from non-league Wealdstone. While Butterworth floundered and was eventually sold to Norwich, Pearce went from strength to strength and became the player Forest fans loved the most and who opposition fans either hated or begrudgingly respected the most. Words simply don't exist to fully express the contribution Pearce made to Forest during his time at the club – there has seldom been a player before or after who could take whole games by the scruff of their necks and change their very nature while the rest of the team were performing lost chicken impressions. Pearce eventually made the England number three shirt his own, and survived the taunts throughout the 1990/91 season after missing a crucial semi-final penalty against Germany at Italia 90. Most people will recall those ghosts being exorcised during the 1996 European Championships when Pearce netted a shoot-out penalty against Spain. Psycho stood by Forest when they were relegated in 1993 despite the threat to his England place but when they went down again in 1997 (after Pearce had had a spell as caretaker manager, first alone and then – allegedly unhappily – in tandem with Dave Bassett) it was a different case, as he was approaching the veteran stage of his career and needed top flight football to retain the attentions of the England manager. He left on a free for Newcastle United and later played for West Ham and Manchester City. He retired in 2002, moving on to the coaching staff at City and becoming boss there in 2005. In 2007, after being sacked by City, he took over the England under-21 coaching role and earned plaudits with his success on the international stage. In 2011 he was announced as manager of the Great Britain Olympic football team, and in 2012 took over as caretaker manager of his national side following the resignation of Fabio Capello.

DAD'S (RED AND WHITE) ARMY

Forest have, since the 1960s, been renowned for their development of young players, but this has not always been the case. Following the club's demotion to the third tier in 1949, manager Billy Walker built a side based on experience in the early-1950s as he sought to lead the Reds back to the top flight, something he achieved in 1957. The oldest ever Forest side is thought to be one that hosted Leeds United on Christmas Day 1953: Harry Walker (37); Geoff Thomas (27), Jack Hutchinson (32); Jack French (28), Horace Gager (36), Jack Burkitt (27); Fred Scott (37), Noel Kelly (three days off 32), Wally Ardron (35), Tommy Capel (31), Alan Moore (26). That gave the team a 'youthful' average age of 32.

CUSTODIAN WOES

Nowadays, most clubs have three or four goalkeepers on their books, so have sufficient cover in case injury or illness strikes. This has of course not always been the case, and there have been a few occasions where Forest have had to resort to plonking an outfield player between the sticks in order to fulfil a fixture. In the early days of the club's history, the goalkeeping position was barely regarded as specialist and a few players played both outfield and in goal, such as Ernest Jardine, Henry Billyeald and the Luntley brothers, Edwin and William. By the start of league football however, most clubs had found a specialist keeper, Forest's first being the fearsome-looking Danny Allsopp. The aforementioned Allsopp was absent for the First Division game against The Wednesday on 15th December 1894 having missed his train. With no reserve keeper, centre-forward Thomas Rose played in goal, and kept a clean sheet. In a reversal of circumstances in 1902, Forest turned up for a game at home to Sunderland a player short, so reserve goalkeeper Alex Newbigging had a turn at inside-right. In the 1900s Jim Iremonger played several games in goal for Forest having previously been the club's regular right- or left-back. Finally, in 1947, Forest's custodian Laurie Platts was unable to secure his day release from the army for a Second Division fixture on 29th January. With Forest's other keepers Reg Savage and Gren Roberts unavailable, forward Tom Johnston pulled on the green jersey. Forest lost the game 3-2.

BROTHERLY UNLOVE

On 27th March 1909 the latest local derby between Forest and Notts County took place at the City Ground. A crowd of 14,000 turned up to see Forest win thanks to a penalty from Enoch "Knocker" West. They also saw something perhaps unique – in goal for Forest was Jim Iremonger, and in goal for Notts was his brother, Albert. Some decades later, on 22nd October 1980, Forest played Leeds United at the City Ground. Forest's left-back was Frank Gray, while Leeds' left-back was his older brother, Eddie.

ON YER BIKE

A fantastic prize was offered to the scorer of the first goal in the 1898 FA Cup Final between Forest and Derby – a brand new bicycle. The bike was won by Forest's Arthur Capes – and the irony that his prize was given to him by Raleigh, who of course were based in Nottingham city centre, was probably not lost on him.

LOANERS

While almost every Forest team since 2000 has featured at least one player on loan from other clubs, the concept of loan players remains a relatively recent one. The first ever loanee for the Reds was David Hollins, a Welsh international goalkeeper who joined the club in an emergency exchange for Duncan McKenzie in 1969 after Forest's regular custodian, Alan Hill, had broken his arm. Next up was David Sunley, who played one game for Forest in 1975 on loan from Sheffield Wednesday, then Colin Barrett from Manchester City who joined permanently in the summer of 1976, and Larry Lloyd who was signed as defensive cover in the same year from Coventry City before joining on a permanent basis a month or so later. Charlie George tried to convince Brian Clough of his fitness in 1980 with a view to a permanent move from Southampton but despite scoring against Barcelona in the Super Cup he was not granted a full transfer. Since 1980 well over 50 players have walked into the City Ground for the temporary feel of a garibaldi shirt, some of whom will forever be remembered with fondness (Richard Gough, John Terry, Robbie Blake, Ben Olsen, Darren Huckerby, Nicky Shorey and Adlène Guedioura, to pick a random handful), others (Francis Benali, Adam Proudlock, Michael Stewart and James Henry as examples) not so much.

THINGS CAN ONLY GET BETTER

The period up to the First World War was perhaps the worst in Forest's history. Barely kept afloat, the club only survived due to several committee members putting their hands into their own pockets. Forest regularly finished around the bottom of the Football League and in 1913 suffered the indignity of 14 successive defeats. After beating Bristol City 4-1 on 15th March, the club's record then went as follows: Bradford Park Avenue (H 1-2), Birmingham (A 0-2), Bradford Park Avenue (A 1-3), Huddersfield Town (H 0-1), Leeds City (A 0-1), Grimsby Town (H 1-2), Bury (A 0-2), Fulham (H 2-4), Leicester Fosse (H 1-3), Wolves (H 1-3), Leicester Fosse (A 1-5), Hull (A 0-1), Barnsley (H 0-2), and Bury (A 0-1). Finally, on 4th October, a John Derrick goal secured a 1-1 draw at home to Huddersfield to stop the rot. It took another fortnight before Forest beat Blackpool 3-0 at home to record their first victory for over seven months.

WORST DEBUT EVER

In 1959, with Forest on the way to the FA Cup Final, and having had to play eight cup ties in the space of two months (as well as four league games), boss Billy Walker gave some of his senior players a rest at home to Birmingham City on 7th March. Out went Jack Burkitt, Bob McKinlay and Johnny Quigley, and in came the experienced Bill Morley, plus reserves Peter Watson and Billy Younger. Also out went "Chick" Thomson, and in his place for a Forest debut came Willie Fraser, an Australian-born Scottish keeper who had been a regular for Sunderland and had won two caps for Scotland before joining Forest. Fraser had a busy day, picking the ball out of the net seven times as Birmingham romped to an embarrassing 7-1 win. Fraser would only play one more game – at Cup Final opponents Luton Town – for Forest before retiring, and Luton won 5-1 with future Forest boss Allan Brown scoring four. Almost rivalling this is Mick Harby, who played three games for Forest in 1967/68 and conceded 15 – 3-0 v Sunderland, 6-1 at Wolves and 6-1 at Liverpool, although press reports at the time put the blame for these heavy defeats at the feet of Forest's leaky defence, rather than Harby's ineptitude.

HELLO AND GOODBYE

Brian Clough was famed for some baffling decisions, and the Forest career of Asa Hartford was one of them. A busy midfielder, Hartford was signed in June 1979 for £400,000 as a direct replacement for Archie Gemmill, who had left the club for Birmingham City, allegedly angry at having to sit out the 1979 European Cup Final on the bench. Hartford slotted straight into the side in Gemmill's usual number eight shirt, and played in three games, against Ipswich, Stoke and Coventry, Forest winning all three. As Forest prepared for a League Cup tie against Blackburn, Hartford was told to pack his bags for Goodison Park, as Everton had offered £450,000 for him, which Forest accepted. Hartford had lasted 63 days as a Nottingham Forest player.

EMERGENCY KEEPERS

Before the advent of substitute goalkeepers, should the number one be injured the only way a match could continue was if a side's outfield player donned the keeper's jersey. This happened to Forest on a few occasions – with mixed results. In October 1973 Jim Barron went off injured in a game at Blackpool after 26 minutes. Striker John Galley went between the sticks and helped the side pull off a creditable 2-2 draw. In September 1975 young keeper John Middleton went off just before half-time with a broken nose. Winger Ian Bowyer took on the keeping mantle and kept a clean sheet as Forest won 1-0 – the goal scored by George Lyall, who came on for Middleton. Less successful was Neil Webb, who replaced Hans Segers after just 13 minutes of a game at West Ham in September 1985. Forest were already two down and despite Webb's "efforts" were four behind after an hour before Johnny Metgod and Nigel Clough pulled goals back. Manager Brian Clough was less than enthused over Webb's display, and suggested the young midfielder should never be allowed on a cricket field.

NOT NOTTINGHAM

Following a debate that had emerged over the past few seasons, a rather odd suggestion was proposed at the end of the 1973/74 season that the word "Nottingham" be dropped from the name of Nottingham Forest Football Club. Happily, the suggestion was voted down at the club's AGM.

STUART THE SPARKY

Buyers of the Forest matchday programme at the start of the 1986/87 campaign may have been tempted by the services of "Stuart Pearce, Electrician", who offered free estimates, repairs, maintenance and complete household rewires, with all work guaranteed. Incredibly, this was actually a genuine advert offering the electrical knowledge of the club's left-back. Despite an encouraging year in the top flight, Pearce still remained unconvinced of his continuing career and decided to keep 'in the know' with his former trade. It is doubtful, five years later, as Forest's captain and England's regular number three, that Pearce was still offering to sort out people's electricity issues.

MY BALL!

A potentially ugly dilemma was averted following Forest's match at Chelsea in September 1986, in which Neil Webb and Garry Birtles both scored hat-tricks to help the club record a 6-2 victory. Traditionally of course, a hat-trick scorer is awarded the ball after the game. Happily, by a fluky coincidence, two match balls had been used during the game as the original had had to be replaced midway through, allowing both Webb and Birtles to take their expected souvenir back home to mark their achievements.

LOCAL LAD DONE GOOD

Forest advertised their forthcoming hosting of an under-15 international between England and Switzerland in April 1987 as an opportunity to witness the progress of a former Nottingham City Boys representative, of who big things were forecast. The Sandfield School youngster had scored three goals in his three games to date for his country, and had already signed an associate schoolboy agreement with Arsenal. His name was Andy Cole. What ever became of him?

TWO FOR THE PRICE OF ONE

In 1980 the German newspaper *Bild-Zeituing* (translated as Picture Newspaper) reported upon Nottingham Forest's signing of two new strikers, those being Ward (Brighton) and Hove (Albion). Brighton's Peter Ward spent almost two seasons at Forest. Hove's period as a Red never quite seemed to get off the ground.

DEAL OR NO DEAL

Footballers can be fickle fiends. In the early 1960s Forest's manager Johnny Carey agreed terms with Blackburn Rovers for their England full-back Keith Newton, only for Newton's wife to decide she didn't want to move from Lancashire, hence scuppering the deal. A later call from Newton suggesting he was prepared to move after all turned out to be a hoax. A few years later the Manchester City striker Francis Lee turned down a move to the City Ground on the basis that he wasn't prepared to either move to the East Midlands or travel down from his home in Lancashire for training. Forest accepted his decision in good faith, then Lee joined Derby County in 1974.

AMATEUR!

Probably the last true amateur to play for Nottingham Forest was the legendary goalkeeper Harry Sharratt. Sharratt was a schoolteacher who played for the dominant non-league side Bishop Auckland. He played for the love of the game, refusing to give up his well-paid day job to turn professional despite many experts proclaiming him to be one of the best custodians going. Sharratt was called in by Billy Walker in February 1958 to give "Chick" Thomson a rest and kept a clean sheet at home to Portsmouth. Sharratt, who made similar 'guest' appearances for Blackpool and Oldham Athletic and appeared for Great Britain at the 1956 Olympics, passed away in Lancaster on 19th August 2002.

THE ARMY GAME

On 24th October 1945, Forest met and were defeated by one of their strangest opponents of all time, the British Army. With the Second World War drawing to a close, British club sides at the time would show their support for troops still stationed overseas by sending teams to play combined squads made up of professional footballers who were still in the services. The game was against a Rhine Army XI and was played at Flensburg, near the Danish frontier. Forest lost the game 4-1, with Tom North scoring the Reds' consolation goal late in the match. The Army XI's goals came from the Arsenal centre-forward Reg Lewis, who scored a hat-trick, and Partick Thistle's Peter McKennan.

THE BORROWED XI

This is a team made up of players who played for Forest while on loan from other clubs. Players who were on loan and then subsequently joined Forest, such as Larry Lloyd, Lee Camp and Dexter Blackstock, are not included.

1   Russell Hoult .... (West Bromwich Albion, 2005/06)
2   Ben Olsen .... (DC United, 2000/01)
3   Nicky Shorey .... (Aston Villa, 2009/10)
4   Matthew Upson ....(Arsenal, 2000/01)
5   John Terry .... (Chelsea, 1999/00)
6   Nick Barmby .... (Leeds United, 2003/04)
7   Aaron Ramsey ....(Arsenal, 2010/11)
8   Charlie George ....(Southampton 1980/81)
9   Darren Huckerby............................. (Manchester City, 2002/03)
10 Ian Wright....................................(West Ham United, 1999/00)
11 Robbie Blake ....(Bradford City, 2000/01)

FEARED BY THE BAD! LOVED BY THE GOOD!

Despite there (allegedly) being two teams in Nottingham, Forest – by dint of their perceived association with Sherwood Forest (although of course the club were named after their original home, the Forest Recreation Ground) – have been the Nottingham side far more closely linked with the legend of Robin Hood. For a short spell a cartoon version of Robin Hood (as drawn in the *Nottingham Evening Post*), known in some quarters as the Jolly Forester, formed the club's badge, and for over 40 years the teams would run onto the pitch at the start of games to the theme tune of the ATV television series *The Adventures of Robin Hood* as sung by Dick James. This was dropped after the turn of the millennium for a five-minute montage of Prokofiev's Dance of the Knights, Born Slippy by Underworld and Pjanoo by Erik Prydz. In 2006 the club re-acknowledged its connection with the legendary outlaw and his band of merry men by playing the theme tune to the modern BBC *Robin Hood* TV series as the players ran out, then in 2011 unveiled an all-black away kit with a shoulder of what was described as "Sherwood Green". Sherwood the Bear was also the name of the club's longest-serving (and many would say, most popular) mascot in the 1990s and 2000s.

COLOURFUL STUFF

Forest are one of the few clubs to retain their original colours throughout their entire history. The original committee meeting that formed the side decreed the club's main colour to be "garibaldi" red, in honour of the Italian patriot Giuseppe Garibaldi, and red it has been ever since. The red shirts have almost always been matched with white shorts, aside from 1892 to 1899 when they were dark blue. Socks have always been red as well, other than two brief flirtations with black. Black trim began to creep into Forest's home shirts in 1986 but disappeared in 1998, hopefully never to be seen again. As for away kits, Forest's second choice has virtually always been plain white shirts, apart from the 1920s when they had a red hoop. In the 1960s Forest seemed just as likely to turn up to colour-clash games in blue shirts. It wasn't really until 1976/77 that Forest adopted a true away kit, yellow with a single white, blue-bordered stripe that aped the design Luton Town had at the time. This lasted one season until replaced by an all-yellow strip with blue trim, which largely remained the norm until 1986 when a simpler kit of white shirts and either red or black shorts came to be adopted. By the early-1990s Forest's kits had reached the nadir – the home shirt was covered in nasty black patches and the yellow away shirt had a "pattern" that looked as if a four-year-old had been let loose on it with a box of felt-tipped pens. Since then away kits have been as typically random as at any other club, from ill-advised Brazil replicas, black and blue stripes, kits that looked like they had been pinched from the crew of the Enterprise in *Star Trek*, and shirts uncomfortably resembling those sported by rivals such as Derby County.

HE PACKS SOME PUNCH

It would have taken a brave opposition forward to head a cross while Forest's goalkeeper of the second half of the 1920s, Len Langford, was between the sticks. Langford was also a proficient boxer, and had been the middleweight champion of the Household Brigade in 1920 and 1921. Langford later appeared in the 1933 FA Cup Final for Manchester City, notable for being the first FA Cup Final where players wore numbered shirts. Langford conceded three goals while sporting 22 on his back.

THE BRIAN CLOUGH TROPHY

In 2007, officials from Forest and Derby met with representatives from the Brian Clough Memorial Fund, along with Nigel Clough and his mother, Barbara, and together they established the idea of the Brian Clough Trophy, a cup to be awarded to the winners of any competitive fixture between Forest and Derby County. This was in honour of the great man himself, who had managed both clubs so magnificently. The first fixture was actually a specially-arranged friendly in which all proceeds went to charity.

31st July 2007 to 29th August 2009: DERBY COUNTY

31st July 2007 Derby 2 Forest 0 (Friendly)
2nd November 2008 Derby 1 Forest 1 (Championship)
23rd January 2009 Derby 1 Forest 1 (FA Cup fourth round)
4th February 2009 Forest 2 Derby 3 (FA Cup fourth round replay)
21st February 2009 Forest 1 Derby 3 (Championship)

29th August 2009 to 30th January 2010: FOREST

29th August 2009 Forest 3 Derby 2 (Championship)

30th January 2010 to 29th December 2010: DERBY COUNTY

30th January 2010 Derby 1 Forest 0 (Championship)

29th December 2010 to 17th September 2011: FOREST

29th December 2010 Forest 5 Derby 2 (Championship)
22nd January 2011 Derby 0 Forest 1 (Championship)

17th September 2011 to date: DERBY COUNTY

17th September 2011 Forest 1 Derby 2 (Championship)
13th March 2012 Derby 1 Forest 0 (Championship)

Forest and Derby had been meeting competitively in football for years before the creation of this competition, most famously in the 1898 FA Cup Final at Crystal Palace which Forest won 3-1. At the time of writing it is Forest who have been the more successful in competitive meetings between the two clubs, winning 36 games in comparison to Derby's 32, with 21 draws, although if you include unofficial first class meetings between the teams it's Derby who have the edge, winning 45 games to Forest's 43.

THE WALLY WITH THE BROLLY

When the then-Forest chairman Nigel Doughty secured the signing of former England coach Steve McClaren in June 2011, it was considered by many to be something of a coup. Eager to rebuild his bruised reputation in English football after failing to guide England to the 2008 European Championships, McClaren and Forest seemed a likely fit, with McClaren's reputation for working with young players melding nicely with a promising crop of talent on the verge of graduating from Forest's Academy. However, the reality swiftly became one of a fracturing marriage, with McClaren's repeated unhappiness at the club's inability to secure players in the transfer market echoing the comments of the boss he replaced at the City Ground, Billy Davies. The rumours were that McClaren was so desperate to secure one player, Newcastle United winger Wayne Routledge, that he was himself prepared to make up the shortfall from his own pocket in the wages Routledge asked for in comparison to those the club were prepared to offer. After just two league wins in eight games, both against struggling opposition, the writing was on the wall following a dreadful 5-1 loss at Burnley. One final defeat, 3-1 at home to Birmingham after Forest had led for an hour then capitulated embarrassingly, added the full stop. Further rumours hinted McClaren had at least written his resignation letter no matter the result against Birmingham, as the Forest board had refused to sanction loan moves for Lloyd Dyer and Michael Kightly. It was soon confirmed that McClaren was on his way, while Doughty also announced he was standing down as Forest chairman.

MORE MEDALS THAN GAMES

Ex-England goalkeeper Chris Woods never made a league appearance for Nottingham Forest despite being on the books of the club for over three years, yet in that time managed to secure two winners' medals. Firstly, he played and starred in the 1978 League Cup Final against Liverpool as regular keeper Peter Shilton was cup-tied (Woods had deputised for Shilton in every round of the competition except the second), then, over a year later he received a European Cup medal as a non-playing substitute as Forest beat Malmö FF 1-0 in the Olympiastadion, Munich, in May 1979. This was Woods' final involvement for the club, as he was sold to Queens Park Rangers later that summer.

AS LONG AS HE'S NOT WELSH

Despite being manager of Nottingham Forest for nearly two decades, and despite signing enough players to fill at least a dozen team sheets, Brian Clough failed to sign one single Welsh-born player during his tenure. The only Welshman to play for Clough while he was Forest boss was defender David Jones, who had been signed by Clough's predecessor Allan Brown, and was sent packing to Norwich City after half a season. Forest had several great Welsh players before Clough, such as Edwin Hughes, Grenville Morris, Terry Hennessey and Ronnie Rees, and have had several since, such as David Phillips, Rob Earnshaw and Chris Gunter, so this paucity of men from the valleys during those vibrant Cloughie years does seem a tad peculiar.

IT WOULDN'T HAPPEN TODAY

Imagine this – Nottingham Forest had just won the FA Cup at Crystal Palace, beating their deadliest rivals, Derby County. Called together for a traditional post-win photo-call, the photographer asked nicely if the Forest players wouldn't mind changing into Derby County's shirts, as the resulting photograph would look much better if they did so because Forest won the cup playing in red shirts and dark blue shorts. The Forest players agreed – so the only photo of Forest's triumphant 1898 Cup-winning team sees them wearing the shirts of the team they'd just defeated. If that sounds perverse, how about the 1933 FA Cup Final in which numbered shirts were worn for the first time? The FA provided two kits, one white and one red, so Manchester City took to the field in one more suited to their rivals United. The red-shirted Manchester City side lost the final 3-0.

CORMACK – COR! SACKED!

Brian Clough's 44 days in charge of Leeds United must have seemed like a lifetime to ex-Forest forward Peter Cormack, who in December 2000 was sacked after only ten days in charge at the then Scottish Third Division leaders Cowdenbeath. Cormack, who had replaced future Scotland boss Craig Levein, and who blamed 'player power' for his demise, left (after a meeting with the chairman at the local hamburger van) the "Blue Brazil" with the spotless playing record of P0 W0 D0 L0 F0 A0.

FOREST THE GIANT KILLERS #2

Forest spent most of the 1920s and 1930s kicking around the middle of the Second Division, so it was quite fortunate that the side embarked on frequent cup runs to entertain their otherwise uninspired fans (in those days the cup was considered more important than the league, anyhow). In 1930 the club undertook one of those such runs, taking the scalp of top flight Sunderland along the way. After hammering Rotherham United 5-0 in the third round, and easing past Fulham at the City Ground in the fourth, the Reds journeyed to Roker Park on 15th February 1930 to take on Sunderland. In truth, Sunderland were not having the best of seasons, battling with seven or so other sides to avoid relegation, but they were still fancied to turn over their mid-table second tier opponents. However, Forest came back down from the north-east with a 2-2 draw, both their goals coming from outside-left Billy Dickinson. The replay at Nottingham four days later went even better for the Reds as they triumphed 3-1, with goals from Jack Scott, Leo Loftus and Noah Burton. The reward was a quarter-final tie against the current champions and league leaders, Sheffield Wednesday. Forest were very much the underdogs again but provided a major shock in holding the Owls to a 2-2 draw at the City Ground in what most Forest fans adjudged to be the side's finest performance for many a year. A crowd of 49,166 turned up to watch a fiercely contested game, with Jack Allen and Ellis Rimmer scoring for Wednesday, Dickinson and Loftus for the Reds. An even more numerous crowd of 59,205 turned up for the replay at Hillsborough, and this time Wednesday proved too good for the Reds, winning 3-1 with Allen, Harry Burgess and Jimmy Seed scoring for the Owls, and Burton replying for Forest. Wednesday went on to retain their league title but were knocked out of the FA Cup by Huddersfield Town at the semi-final stage, whereas Forest finished tenth in the Second Division.

JASON LEE WITHE

Was it some weird echo from the future that persuaded Forest's late-1970s rambunctious centre-forward Peter Withe to christen his son with the first names 'Jason Lee' in honour of Forest's future, giving-his-all, pineapple-headed forward, or just coincidence? We perhaps, shall never know.

TRANSFER FLOPS #2

Forest boss Frank Clark had money to burn during the summer of 1995 following the record-breaking £8.5m sale of Stan Collymore to Liverpool. If he had burnt £1.8m of it instead of splashing that amount out on one-cap Italian international striker Andrea Silenzi, most observers may have agreed that it would have been a much more beneficial use of nearly two million quid. Announced as the first Italian to play in the Premiership, Silenzi now vies with the likes of Tomas Brolin, Ali Dia and Marco Boogers as the most disastrous top flight signing ever. In nearly three years, the languid striker netted around £1.2m in wages, yet scored only two goals, in cups against footballing behemoths Oxford United and Bradford City. Famously, *Match of the Day* pundit Alan Hansen, upon seeing one of Silenzi's displays of glorious ineptitude, stated: "If he is an Italian international then the other 22 players must have been injured." In 1997 Silenzi was packed off back to his native land and joined Venezia on loan, then refused to return when that was up. Not one red tear was shed, especially not by the Forest manager Dave Bassett who tore up the Italian's contract on the spot.

TWO CAPS IN ONE DAY

Larry Lloyd perhaps typified precisely the kind of career-resurrection that became second nature to Brian Clough and Peter Taylor during their management days. Signed by Bill Shankly for Liverpool in 1969 from Bristol Rovers, Lloyd was a regular at Anfield for four seasons, winning three England caps and forming a no-nonsense defensive partnership with Tommy Smith. The wheels fell off in 1974 when injury saw Lloyd lose his place to Phil Thompson, and he was sold to Coventry for £240,000. By October 1976 Lloyd couldn't even get into the Coventry team, and was offloaded to Forest for a bargain £60,000. It was a move that rekindled his career, and his new partnership with Kenny Burns became one of legend. By 1980 Lloyd's resurrection was complete as he'd just won Forest's Player of the Season award and earned a recall to the England side, eight years after his last cap. Unfortunately, Lloyd's display against Wales in a 4-1 defeat was hardly glorious, and only semi-accurately, Clough quipped: "Larry Lloyd got two caps today, his first and his last." Lloyd never played for England again.

HE WEARS THE RED, HE WEARS THE WHITE

Players who turn up to matches against clubs they've previously played for are always guaranteed a rousing cheer and a warm round of applause. This friendliness is frequently encountered at the City Ground, no more so than in games between Forest and Derby in which players take the field for the Rams having previously sported the red of Forest, or vice versa. This has applied to no less than 30 post-war players, from Stewart Imlach to the last man to move between the two rivals, Nathan Tyson. In the 1960s a whole flux of players deserted Forest for Brian Clough's Baseball Ground revolution: Alan Hinton, Terry Hennessey, Henry Newton and Frank Wignall (via Wolves – and almost, Ian Storey-Moore). The tide turned in 1975 once Clough had arrived at the City Ground, with John McGovern, John O'Hare, Archie Gemmill and Colin Todd all signing for Forest after playing for Clough at Derby. Later added to that list was Charlie George, who was signed for Derby by Dave Mackay and spent a month on loan at Forest under Clough. In 1982 Peter Shilton left Forest and turned up at Derby County in 1987 after a spell at Southampton. Most controversially, John Robertson was signed by Peter Taylor for Derby in 1983 before Clough had time to negotiate a new contract with the portly wing wizard. The transfer permanently ended the relationship between the two great men. Another European Cup winner, Kenny Burns, had a spell at Derby between 1984 and 1985. Completing the post-war list of players to have played for both sides are John Middleton, Steve Sutton, Lee Camp, Gary Charles, Darren Wassall, Gary Mills, Terry Curran, Steve Hodge, Glyn Hodges, Darryl Powell, Lars Bohinen, Mikkel Beck, Dean Saunders, Dexter Blackstock, Rob Earnshaw, Marcus Tudgay, Kris Commons and Nathan Tyson.

CAMP'S CALAMITY

Lee Camp is generally regarded as Forest's finest keeper since Dave Beasant, having joined the club in 2008, initially on loan from QPR, but he holds one distinctive record that is also slightly dubious. In 2007 Camp was playing for the England under-21s against Italy and conceded a goal to Giampaolo Pazzini after just 25 seconds and in doing so, conceded the first goal to be scored during a professional match held at the new Wembley Stadium. The game ended 3-3.

NUMBER FOUR IS...

Des Walker. Primarily, the coolest defender ever to pull on a garibaldi red shirt. Walker's ability to judge instantly the situation whenever a striker pounded towards him, then whip the ball off the attacker's toe without fuss and with perfect timing bordered on the preternatural. Even when it was two against Walker, Forest fans would simply pick up their matchday programmes and read an interesting article about Steve Sutton's Christmas, safe in the knowledge that an opposition goal remained unlikely. The pacey defender was born in London on 26th November 1965 and was picked up from Tottenham Hotspur after he'd been dubbed too small. He broke into the team in 1984, initially as a right-back, but after the sale of Paul Hart and a long-term injury to Chris Fairclough, Walker took his natural place in the centre and never looked back. The Forest side of the late-1980s saw the club rise back to being one of the country's elite, with Walker at the forefront of the many talents it had been assembled from. England honours followed, and Walker's performance for his country in Italia 90 cemented his place as one of Europe's classiest defenders. Many of the continent's top sides came hunting, and once it was disclosed a clause in Walker's last contract meant he could move abroad for £1.5m (about a fifth of his true worth at the time), interest rose and in the summer of 1992 Walker joined Sampdoria. Brian Clough had allegedly fallen out with the youngster touted as Walker's replacement, Darren Wassall, who was also sold, and Forest were relegated the next season. At Sampdoria Walker was often played as a left-back by his manager, Sven-Goran Eriksson, and also suffered an injury that affected his pace. He returned to England with Sheffield Wednesday for £2.7m after just one season in Italy, and immediately became the cornerstone of the Owls' defence. Despite that slight loss in pace Walker remained one of the top defenders in England but somehow his England career stalled and ceased at 59 caps. He left Wednesday in 2001 and after a year out of the professional game was recruited by Paul Hart for his second spell at Forest. He played a further two seasons, his presence a boon for his rookie defensive partner Michael Dawson, before finally retiring in 2004 to join Forest's coaching staff. Walker left the club for the last time in January 2005 upon the appointment of Gary Megson as boss.

A CHANCE FOR REVENGE?

There are extra snippets of interest in two of Forest's most significant games in their history. In the 1959 FA Cup Final which Forest won 2-1 against Luton Town, among the Hatters' team that day was future Forest manager Allan Brown. Also, in 1975, Brian Clough's first game in charge at Forest, and the first FA Cup tie against Tottenham that Forest also won, Spurs' right-back that day was another future Forest manager, Joe Kinnear.

CLOUGHIE'S FIRST SIGNING

Brian Clough's first signing for Nottingham Forest was not, as many believe, John McGovern (along with John O'Hare, both rescued after following Clough to his Elland Road nightmare), but Bertram "Bert" Bowery, who was signed on 24th January 1975. Centre-forward Bowery was snapped up from Worksop Town after playing for Ilkeston Town and Clifton All-Whites. He scored twice on his league debut, but that turned out to be only one of two league games he played for the Reds, although he also played in the FA Cup and Anglo-Scottish Cup. Bowery left the club in 1977 and enjoyed a spell in the States. At the time of writing, Bowery's son, Jordan, is carving out a successful football career of his own at Chesterfield.

THE FAGS ON THE BUS GO OUT OUT OUT

One of the measures Brian Clough enforced on the team straight from the off was the banning of smoking on the team bus. This was allegedly especially annoying to the chain-smoking defender Paddy Greenwood, who was known to sneak a crafty fag whenever the opportunity arose.

THANKS FRANK, THANKS

Frank Wignall, who Forest signed from Everton in 1963, enjoyed a fine international debut on 18th November 1964 for England, scoring twice against Wales in the Home Internationals to help secure a 2-1 win. It remains the best international debut for a Forest man. Frank played for England again three weeks later in a friendly against Holland, but was never selected again. He went on to play for Wolverhampton Wanderers, Derby County, and Mansfield Town.

OUR JIMMY

The third member of the massively successful Clough/Taylor dream team was undoubtedly the hugely likeable Scot, Jimmy Gordon, who was Forest's first team trainer between 1975 and 1981. Gordon's appearance on the Forest field to wield his alchemy with the magic sponge was always cheered by the Reds' faithful along with the song "Jimmy, give us a wave, Jimmy, Jimmy, give us a wave". Gordon's true contribution to Forest's success must never be forgotten, as he was as much a repairer of footballer's bodies as he was a repairer of the frail egos battered by frequent Clough outbursts. While Clough was perhaps the bad cop, and Taylor the good cop, it was Gordon's role to play the stern but fair father to Forest's crop of young talents. Gordon had enjoyed a fine career himself, as a wing-half at Newcastle and Middlesbrough, and it had been at Ayresome Park that Clough had first met him. After moving into coaching at Middlesbrough and then Blackburn Rovers, Gordon picked up his phone one day in 1969 to hear Clough asking him to join him at Derby County. After a little persuasion Gordon accepted, and cemented the final piece in the Clough/Taylor/Gordon trinity, although Gordon's name is almost always forgotten when considering everything Brian Clough and Peter Taylor achieved together. The pair themselves never forgot, and even shoved Gordon out in front to lead Forest on to the pitch for the 1980 League Cup Final against Wolves. Jimmy retired at the end of the 1980/81 season. He passed away in Derby, in August 1996, at the age of 82.

THE BROKEN SCORER

Between the reigns of Joe McDonald and Peter Hindley as Forest's right-back, the man in possession of the number two shirt was Joe Wilson, signed from Workington in 1961. Wilson was a player with pace and an accurate crossing ability, and who only scored once for Forest and in unusual circumstances. In October 1964, in a match at Stoke City, Wilson suffered an injury. These were the days before substitutes, so as the theory went an injured player was better than no player at all, and Wilson was left to hobble around as a makeshift centre-forward. The battling Wilson still had enough about him to net, earning Forest a point in a 1-1 draw.

THE GROUNDS OF NOTTINGHAM FOREST

Nottingham Forest did not really have a regular home for their football endeavours until 1883. Their initial home was the Forest Recreation Ground and they played the majority of their matches there until 1878, when games began to be played at the Castle Ground in the Meadows. As football gained in popularity as crowd numbers began to swell, for more important games Forest played at Trent Bridge. In 1883 Forest moved to a purpose-built field at Lenton, known as the Parkside Ground, their first game being against Small Heath Alliance which Forest won 3-2 with goals by Tinsley Lindley, Sam Widdowson and Fred Earp. After just two seasons at the Parkside (where the club were never happy due to the slope of the pitch and its inability to drain water), Forest were on the move again, this time to the Gregory Ground as used by Lenton United Cricket Club, adjacent to Wollaton Park. They stayed in Lenton until 1890/91, by which time league football had been invented (although Forest were playing in the Northern or Football Alliance as they initially refused to submit to the idea of professionalism). With Notts County playing in the more illustrious Football League and attracting larger crowds at Trent Bridge, Forest felt inclined to move closer to the city centre, and acquired what was then called Woodward's Field, to be renamed the Town Ground. The official opening of the new ground was on 2nd October but only after Notts County had protested (as they had a league game with Bolton on the same day) and the original opponents, Football League side Wolves, had been ordered not to play. Instead, the famous Scottish amateur side, Queen's Park, were coaxed down and 3,500 turned up to witness Forest's 4-2 victory. The Town Ground served as their home until 1898, by which time Nottingham Forest had evolved into one of the country's top sides, having just won the FA Cup. Flushed with cash, the club commissioned the building of a brand new stadium on the banks of the River Trent. The ground was named the City Ground and the club have been there ever since. In June 2007 Forest announced that they were to leave the City Ground to move to a proposed new stadium in Gamston, towards the south of the city. This plan depended upon England being awarded the role of hosts of the 2018 World Cup, and therefore was shelved when Fifa unexpectedly announced that the competition was to be held in Russia.

ON THE BANKS OF THE TRENT... THE CITY GROUND CIRCA 1998

AND THE GOALS DOTH FLOW

It's a mark that a striker expects to reach – double figures in goals each season, possibly a dozen or at least 15. In the 1988/89 season Forest set new records in that no less than seven members of their first team squad reached double figures in all competitions, and not all of them were strikers. Those net-bulgers were Nigel Clough (20), Lee Chapman (18), Neil Webb (14), Garry Parker (12), Stuart Pearce (11) and both Steve Hodge and Tommy Gaynor (ten). In total, Forest recorded a grand total of 113 goals in all competitions.

THE HURRICANE BLOWS IN

In 1975 the Sportsman's Club arranged a brief, three-day snooker tournament between four of the world's top players: John Spencer, Dennis Taylor, Graham Miles and Alex "Hurricane" Higgins. These were the days before most people had a colour TV and therefore before professional snooker enjoyed the television boom of the late-1970s and most of the 1980s. The inclusion of Higgins was most appropriate, as Forest had previously had two players with that name of their books, although they were both better known by their nickname of "Sandy". The first "Sandy" Higgins was Forest's hugely successful striker of the era just before the club entered league football in the 1890s. The second was the son of the first, and played for the club for two seasons in the early-1920s. Back to the snooker, the Hurricane was hammered in his match against Miles 8-1, while Spencer defeated Taylor 5-4. In the final, Spencer beat Miles 10-7.

SHILTON IN OPPOSITION

On tour in Denmark in July 1979, Forest were playing against Holstebro and finding things a little too easy, leading 4-0 at half-time thanks to a hat-trick from Martin O'Neill and one further strike from Kenny Burns. At the break Peter Taylor came up with the novel idea of switching goalkeepers to give Forest a bit more of a challenge, so the Reds played the second half having to beat Peter Shilton to score. The notion obviously worked, as Forest could only draw the second half 1-1, John Robertson having the joy of planting a penalty past his club-mate.

YOU'LL NEVER SCORE, DES WALKER

While renowned at patrolling his own penalty area, for defender Des Walker the opposition box was as far distant, most of the time, as a foreign country. On New Year's Day 1992, and during Walker's 313th game for the Reds, it happened – Des Walker scored. Forest had been trailing to Luton Town in a league game ever since the opening moments when, with mere seconds to go, Walker was played through and into the penalty area. The crowd let go a mighty roar of expectation that swiftly turned into one of jubilation as Walker smashed the ball home as if he'd been playing up front all his life. To make this event even more unique, the player beaten was Forest goalkeeper Steve Sutton, on loan to the Hatters at the time.

A LITTLE BIT OF TRIVIA

One trivia question almost always guaranteed to fox even the most tenacious Forest expert would be: "Which member of the squad that began the 1977/78 championship-winning season for Forest had scored the most goals the previous term?" While one assumes most Forest fans of that era would plump for either Peter Withe, Tony Woodcock or John Robertson, the correct answer would have been central defender Kenny Burns, who had scored 19 goals for Birmingham City during the 1976/77 season as a centre-forward.

LIKE FATHER, LIKE SON

Forest have had a few father-son combinations throughout their history. The pre-war combination of Alex "Sandy" Higgins and his son, also called Alex, is chronicled elsewhere in this volume. Forest's right-back throughout the 1960s was Peter Hindley, whose father Frank, a speedy forward, enjoyed a brief spell at Forest shortly before the Second World War. Archie Gemmill and his son Scot form probably the most famous father-son combination in Forest's history, amassing over 300 league appearances at the club in combination. Full-back Frank Gray and his son, utility player Andy, both had careers of decent lengths at Forest. Ian Bowyer's son, Gary, was briefly a professional at Forest before joining his father at Hereford United, while Chris Fairclough's son Jordan was also with the club for a while, but got no further than sitting on the bench for one game.

SENT TO COVENTRY

Double transfers are quite unusual, and of the handful of double-deals Forest have been involved with, two have been with the same club, Coventry City. In June 1954, the Sky Blues enquired about the availability of left-winger Colin Collindridge. Forest boss Billy Walker gave the green light, as long as Collindridge's left-sided partner Tommy Capel was included in the deal. The pair spent a couple of reasonably successful seasons at Highfield Road before moving on – Capel to Halifax Town and Collindridge to Bath City. Fast forward to 1985, when Brian Clough snapped up promising centre-half Ian Butterworth from City, then allegedly asked at the last moment if Coventry wouldn't mind chucking in a certain left-back named Stuart Pearce as well.

DOUBLE DOUBLE-BARRELLED

When Ian Storey-Moore made his debut in 1963, it gave rise to the question of whether he was the first double-barrel surnamed player to play for the club. A quick scan of the history books revealed one appearance in 1901 for one Morgan M Morgan-Owen (sadly, the M for his middle name was not another "Morgan", but "Maddox"). Morgan-Owen was a famous amateur player who had played for numerous clubs and who won 11 full caps for Wales between 1879 and 1907. He subsequently served at Gallipoli in the First World War, became president of the Casuals club and master in charge of football at Repton School.

THE CHRISTMAS CRICKETER

Before the 1970s it was not unusual for sportsmen to play both first-class cricket and football, and Forest have had a few such sportsmen in their ranks throughout their history. Leading all-rounder Walter Robins of Middlesex played two games for Forest on Christmas Day 1929 and 1930, and went on to play Test cricket for England on 19 occasions. Right back in the first fledgling days of organised football, Harry Daft, Jim Iremonger, Sam Widdowson and Tinsley Lindley all appeared in first class cricket and also for both Forest and the England football team. One other player who combined the sports was Stuart McMillan, the Derbyshire county cricketer (and later Derby County manager) who played nine games for Forest in the 1927/28 season.

YOU'RE OUT THE ARMY NOW

The Forest matchday programme reported in September 1957 that their young centre-forward Ken Simcoe was now available for selection, after being demobbed from his national service.

DEFENDING CONSISTENTLY

On 3rd November 1956, an injury to right-back Bill Whare brought Jack Hutchinson into the Forest team for a game at Stoke City. The Forest defence for that day was Hutchinson, Geoff Thomas, Bill Morley, Bob McKinlay and Jack Burkitt. In a marvellous display of consistency, that exact defence remained in place for the next 33 league and cup games, until 14th September 1957 when the recovered Whare re-replaced Hutchinson in the number two shirt. The only change to the entire defence during this period was the replacement of custodian Harry Nicholson in goal at the start of the 1957/58 season by the new signing from Chelsea, "Chick" Thomson.

CLOUGH AN UNWELCOME VISITOR

The date of 10th November 1956 was a decent day for Middlesbrough, as they travelled down to Nottingham for a Second Division game with Forest and journeyed back up north with a handsome 4-0 victory to boast about. Especially boastful may have been the youthful striker who had just scored his first senior hat-trick, that man being the shy and retiring future legend that was Brian Clough.

OPENING DAY BLUES

While 12 clubs were tentatively enjoying themselves in the new Football League, Forest's start to the 1888/89 season could barely have been more disastrous. With a friendly against Birmingham St George arranged, of the players assigned to the club for the start of the season, three of them had been unable to get time off work, one was on holiday, and two had chosen instead to help out at Nottingham Rowing Club's regatta. The club hastily assembled a scratch side, only then for three of them to miss the train. Two St George players were handed to Forest so they could fulfil the fixture, while an ex-Notts Rangers player, Bull, was shoved in goal. Not surprisingly, Forest lost the game 7-1.

YOU'D BETTER 'B'-LIEVE IT

A note in the Forest programme for the game against Manchester United in October 1957 congratulated Jim Barrett for his selection for the England B team for a forthcoming fixture, hence becoming the first Forest man to be picked for England since Tommy Graham in 1931. Unfortunately, the validity of the match is somewhat dubious as it was against a "combined Sheffield XI". The club had to wait seven years before their next full England international, Alan Hinton, was selected for a Home International match in October 1964. The England B side was haphazardly resurrected in 1978 and a few Forest players made appearances in it, namely Dave Needham (six caps), Viv Anderson (seven), Justin Fashanu (one), Garry Birtles (one), Peter Ward (one), Peter Davenport (one), Steve Hodge (two), Garry Parker (one), Nigel Clough (three) and Brian Laws (one). Davenport's one cap and Hodge's first appearance came on home turf, in a game against New Zealand at the City Ground in November 1984, in which Hodge scored and Forest keeper Steve Sutton was on the bench.

WITH(E)OUT PETER

Championship-winning sides seldom remain together long, but in the case of Forest's conquering 1977/78 team of all talents, once that season was over that team only played together twice more before one of the component pieces, Peter Withe, was sold. This represented a calculated gamble by Clough and Taylor, who perhaps recognised "Googie" (as he was known among his team-mates, presumably after the actress Googie Withers) was not the number nine to lead Forest on to greater glories. Forest made it known that Withe was available for transfer, and received bids from clubs as diverse as Minnesota Kicks and the Brazilian side Cruzeiro, but only freshly-relegated Newcastle United matched Forest's £200,000 valuation and Withe was sent to St James' Park. For Forest, it was almost a failure as Withe's allegedly-ready replacement, Steve Elliott, found the step up from the reserves too great a jump and floundered. Luckily, second-choice Garry Birtles fared somewhat more successfully. Withe himself went on to gain legendary status at Aston Villa following a £500,000 transfer in 1980 and earned the European glory he missed out on at Forest by scoring the only goal of the 1982 European Cup final between Villa and Bayern Munich.

SCOT-FREE OF INTERNATIONALS

Despite having been formed in 1865, and having had numerous Scots on their books, Forest had to wait until 1958 before a single one of their players gained an international cap for Scotland. The man in question was outside-left Stewart Imlach, who was invited for trials prior to the 1958 World Cup and then capped in games against Hungary, Poland, Yugoslavia and France, the last two in the finals themselves. Since Imlach, Peter Cormack, John Robertson, Archie Gemmill, Kenny Burns, Frank Gray, Scot Gemmill and Gareth Williams have all been selected for the full Scotland international side. In 2005, Imlach's son, the journalist Gary, campaigned for his father and other players to be awarded caps for their selection for Scotland. It was the policy of the Scottish FA at the time of Imlach's selection to only award caps for matches involving England, Wales or Northern Ireland, hence Imlach never received one. In 2006, Imlach was posthumously awarded his cap, having passed away in 2001. Gary Imlach went on to publish a biography on his father Stewart entitled *My Father and Other Working Class Football Heroes* which won the William Hill Sport Book of the Year prize.

LIGHTENING FAST GETAWAY

The first (and so far, only) South African to play for Forest was goalkeeper Arthur Lightening, who played five games for the club in 1958 as an understudy to the regular custodian "Chick" Thomson. He eventually moved to Coventry City in 1959 where he gained a slight reputation as both "a bit of a character" and a firm fan favourite. In 1962 Arthur was signed by Middlesbrough and on his debut generated a sportswriter's dream as he let in six goals against Newcastle United ("Lightening Thunder Struck" was one headline). Lightening was not a success at Middlesbrough and even appeared in court for receiving stolen beer, wine and spirits in his room while staying in a hotel (he was found guilty but given an absolute discharge after charming the judge). After just 14 games for Middlesbrough, Lightening asked for permission to travel to his brother's wedding in May 1963 – and never returned. "I thought it strange that he only booked a single ticket," the travel agent told an investigating journalist. Arthur passed away just before the turn of the millennium.

THE BLINK AND YOU MISSED 'EM XI

This is a team made up of players who have played in Forest's first team – but only just, having made a single start or sub appearance:

1   Karl Darlow............................ (v Crystal Palace, 7th May 2011)
2   John Piekalnietis.............................. (v Arsenal, 26th Dec 1969)
3   Marcus Hall................................ (v Portsmouth, 10th Aug 2002)
4   Steve Burke............(v Ayr, Anglo-Scottish Cup, 20th Oct 1976)
5   Craig Boardman ....(v Bolton, League Cup, 25th Sep 1991)
6   Gary Andrews ....(v Brighton, League Cup, 8th Oct 1986)
7   James Henry.............................. (v Cheltenham, 24th Mar 2007)
8   James Reid...................................... (v Barnsley, 29th Nov 2008)
9   Neil Lyne..................... (v Burnley, League Cup, 10th Oct 1990)
10 Jason Kaminsky ....(v Luton Town, 14th Apr 1992)
11 Ian Kilford .... (v Bolton, 26th Sep 1993)

They consist of a grand total of one full appearance (by Marcus Hall), and ten substitute appearances. Probably the shortest Forest career of all time belongs to James Reid, who came on as substitute against Barnsley in the first minute of injury time, with the referee blowing for time a minute or so later. It was Reid's only appearance for Forest before he was released at the end of the 2008/09 season.

THE LOYAL CLUB SERVANTS XI

1   Mark Crossley ....(1989-2000, 393 games)
2   Viv Anderson..(1974-84, 430 games)
3   Stuart Pearce..(1985-97, 522 games)
4   Bobby McKinlay..(1951-70, 685 games)
5   Steve Chettle ....(1986-99, 526 games)
6   Jack Burkitt...(1947-62, 503 games)
7   Billy Thompson ....(1922-33, 390 games)
8   Ian Bowyer................................. (1973-81, 1982-87, 564 games)
9   Nigel Clough .... (1984-93, 1996-97, 412 games)
10 Grenville Morris.....................................(1898-1913, 460 games)
11 John Robertson........................... (1970-83, 1985-86, 514 games)

A grand total of 5,399 games, or, if you prefer, roughly 485,910 minutes!

WHERE HAVE YOU BEEN?

Brian Clough was never a man to shy away from telling a player he wasn't good enough. Asa Hartford lasted three games as Archie Gemmill's replacement before being packed off to Everton. Irish international John Sheridan fared even worse – signed from Leeds United to replace Neil Webb, Sheridan only played once (and then, allegedly, was not picked by Clough at all but by his assistants Ronnie Fenton and Liam O'Kane, who had been allowed to pick the side for League Cup games that season) before being sold to Sheffield Wednesday. Gary Megson did worse still – his entire Forest playing career consisting of one appearance as an unused substitute in a Uefa Cup tie. There are, however, players who have seemingly been discarded by Clough only to fare better when given a second chance. Left-back Bryn Gunn had made the first team in 1976 for six games, but after playing against Carlisle United on 6th March 1976 had to wait almost four years before his next match against Bolton on 1st March 1980. Gunn would eventually end up playing for Forest 159 times and earning a European Cup winner's medal. Icelandic midfielder Toddy Orlygsson started brightly after his signing from KA Akureyi in 1989 but swiftly seemed to lose his nerve and didn't play for the first team at all between March 1990 and April 1992 before returning a very different player. Most famous of all was Garry Birtles, who was handed his debut in the 1976/77 season against Hull City and failed to impress. He had to wait 18 months for his second chance, against Arsenal in September 1978. It was one he took with some considerable success.

GOAL-SHY FRANK

Frank Clark was Forest's left-back between 1975 and 1979 (although he missed most of the 1977/78 season through injury) and of course later manager and chairman. Frank was notoriously goal-shy, managing 400 games with Newcastle without scoring then over 100 with Forest. Finally, in April 1978, Clark netted, in a league game at Ipswich Town. Oddly, Clark was playing up front at the time, on as substitute for striker Peter Withe. Forest were already 1-0 up, the other goal coming from Paul Mariner who had put through his own net. Forest won 2-0, and it was the only goal Frank scored in his entire career.

NUMBER FIVE IS...

Steve Chettle. One of the most unsung of the unsung heroes of Forest's history, Chettle was a local lad who rose through the ranks and became the regular number five for well over a decade. "Chets" first made the side in 1986, out of position at right-back after Gary Fleming had been injured. He moved to his more natural position once Chris Fairclough and Johnny Metgod had left for Tottenham, and formed a natural partnership with the outstanding Des Walker. While Walker was the guile, Chettle was the grit. Despite a fair proportion of the Forest faithful never being wholly convinced that there weren't better qualifiers for Chettle's position, it was pointed out that you didn't get to play over 500 games for one of Brian Clough's sides if you weren't good enough. Chettle played regularly for Clough, Clark and Bassett, winning a dozen England under-21 caps along the way, until David Platt took over and ended his Forest career, sending him first on loan and then permanently to Barnsley. In 2002 he joined Grimsby Town on then Burton Albion a year later. After 12 months at Burton and a further year at Ilkeston Town Chettle retired from competitive football. He ran a soccer school then returned to Forest as Academy coach to the under-13 side.

JEMMO JABBED

Brian Clough definitely had a way with people, as young striker Nigel Jemson once found out. Signed as a teenager from Preston, Cloughie had gone to watch the reserves at Derby County, and Jemson was playing up front. The youngster, eager to impress, had attempted some fancy step-overs during the first half, but had unfortunately fallen over the ball, twice. Clough nipped down to dressing room at half-time and asked Jemson to stand up. The timid Jemson did so, and Clough punched him in the stomach. "Don't you ever try those fancy tricks again while your mum and dad are in the stand" was Clough's advice.

DOUBLE DOUBLE CLOUGH

In the 2011/12 season, Nigel Clough guided Derby County to their first double over Forest for 40 years. Of course, the last manager to lead the Rams to a league double over the Reds, in 1971/72, was his father, Brian Clough.

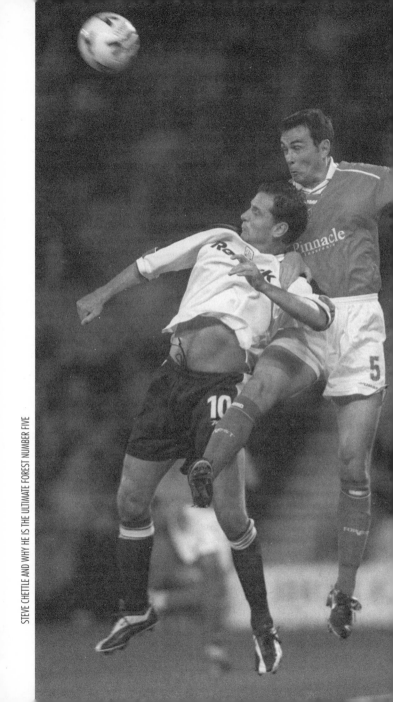

WHAT'S IN A NAME?

In the early-1960s Forest picked up a young winger called Flip Le Flem. Most Forest supporters pondered how he'd gotten such an unusual name until Flip disclosed his real name was actually Richard and he'd no idea where the nickname "Flip" had come from. At the same time a young inside-forward called Bobby Chapman began to emerge into the first team, while in the early-1970s Forest's skipper was the no-nonsense stopper Sammy Chapman. Most casual football supporters might have enquired whether these two players were related, and indeed they were, as they were the same player – "Bobby" became "Sammy" around about the same time he moved from the forward line successfully into defence. In the late-1960s Forest snapped up a young Irishman called Billy O'Kane. He was still being referred to as such by commentators five years later, despite it being known the defender preferred to be known as Liam. Flash forward a decade and Chris Fairclough was by now a regular in Forest's defence, and was known to all as "Chris" despite being christened Courtney Huw Fairclough. Scot "son of Archie" Gemmill suffered frequent mis-spellings of his name as Scott before disclosing he was definitely Scot as his first name was actually Scotland. And finally, the hit-and-miss Forest striker Junior Agogo actually had the first name Manuel, which might have explained why many of his efforts on goal were repeatedly 'fawlty'. Other players in Forest's history who are better known by nicknames than the names their parents gave them include William "Tich" Smith, Robert Albert John "Sailor" Brown, Ronald "Tot" Leverton, and Tom "Tucker" Johnson.

BENNETT'S BIZARRE BOOKING

On 19th January 2008, Forest left-back Julian Bennett received a booking during a league match at Swindon Town. Nothing remarkable in that perhaps, except that Bennett wasn't even on the pitch at the time and played no part in the game. While warming up as a substitute, Bennett spoke a little too harshly to referee Mike Thorpe after a goalmouth scramble in the Forest box led to a few boots flying in. Bennett was not impressed and let the referee know at full volume, and was promptly booked. It's probably the only occasion a Forest player has received a caution without entering the field of play.

THERE'S ONLY TWO GEOFF THOMASES

Forest have had a handful of players throughout their history who have shared their names with players who have represented Nottingham Forest in previous seasons. Alex "Sandy" Higgins of the pre-league days and Alex "Sandy" Higgins of the 1920s were father and son. John "Jack" Armstrong was a stalwart defender for the club between 1905 and 1922, while John "Jack" Armstrong was a reserve goalkeeper who made a few appearances for the club around the turn of the 1960s. Finally, Geoff Thomas (whose actual first name was Gerard but was known to everyone as Geoff) was Forest's regular left-back from the recommencement of football after the Second World War until just before the 1959 FA Cup win, and Geoff Thomas was the ex-England midfielder signed by the club in 1997 whose Reds' career was blighted by injury until his release in 1999.

THE 42

Between November 1977 and November 1978 Nottingham Forest were simply unbeatable in the league and proved it in the simplest way possible – by not losing any games. The previous record of 34 set by Leeds United in 1969/70 was eclipsed during Forest's magnificent run (coincidentally Leeds were the last team to beat Forest prior to it getting going) which came to an end at Anfield as Liverpool won 2-0, virtually a year after it started. The record stood for over a quarter of a century before Arsenal surpassed it in 2004, setting the new benchmark at 49. Forest also lost the record for the longest unbeaten run in the Football League in 2011 when Huddersfield Town went 43 games without defeat in League 1. Forest's unbeaten run was truly a remarkable achievement and full details of it are reproduced here:

26th November 1977 v West Bromwich Albion (H). 0-0 Shilton, Anderson, Barrett, McGovern, Gemmill, O'Neill, Withe, Woodcock, Robertson.
3rd December 1977 v Birmingham City (A). 2-0 (O'Neill, Woodcock). Unchanged team, although Gemmill and O'Neill swapped shirt numbers.
10th December v Coventry City (H). 2-1 (McGovern, O'Neill). Unchanged.

17th December 1977 v Manchester United (A). 4-0 (Woodcock two, Robertson, B Greenhoff OG). Needham in for Lloyd, making his debut.

26th December 1977 v Liverpool (H). 1-1 (Gemmill). Unchanged.

28th December 1977 v Newcastle United (A). 2-0 (McGovern, Needham). Unchanged, Bowyer came on for Withe as a substitute.

31st December 1977 v Bristol C (A). 3-1 (Needham, O'Neill, Woodcock). Unchanged.

2nd January 1978 v Everton (H). 1-1 (Robertson penalty). Unchanged.

14th January 1978 v Derby County (A). 0-0. Unchanged.

21st January 1978 v Arsenal (H). 2-0 (Gemmill, Needham). Unchanged.

4th February 1978 v Wolverhampton Wanderers (H). 2-0 (McGovern, Woodcock). Unchanged.

25th February 1978 v Norwich City (A). 3-3 (Barrett, O'Neill, Withe). Unchanged.

4th March 1978 v West Ham United (H). 2-0 (Needham, Robertson penalty). Shilton, Bowyer, Clark, O'Hare, Needham, Burns, O'Neill, Gemmill, Withe, Woodcock, Robertson.

14th March 1978 v Leicester City (H). 1-0 (Robertson penalty). Anderson in for Withe with Bowyer moving to number nine.

25th March 1978 v Newcastle United (H). 2-0 (Anderson, Robertson penalty). Withe in for Bowyer, Anderson came on for Withe as a substitute.

29th March 1978 v Middlesbrough (A). 2-2 (O'Neill, Woodcock). Bowyer in for Anderson.

1st April 1978 v Chelsea (H). 3-1 (Burns, O'Neill, Robertson penalty). Lloyd in for Needham, Barrett came on for Gemmill as a substitute.

5th April 1978 v Aston Villa (A). 1-0 (Woodcock). Anderson in for Bowyer, Barrett in for Clark.

11th April 1978 v Manchester City (A). 0-0. Unchanged.

15th April 1978 v Leeds United (H). 1-1 (Withe). Shilton, Barrett, Clark, McGovern, Lloyd, Burns, O'Neill, Gemmill, Withe, Bowyer, Robertson.

18th April 1978 v Queens Park Rangers (H). 1-0 (Robertson penalty). Unchanged.

22nd April 1978 v Coventry City (A). 0-0. Shilton, Anderson, Barrett, O'Hare, Needham, Burns, O'Neill, Bowyer, Withe, Gemmill, Robertson.

25th April 1978 v Ipswich Town (A). 2-0 (Clark, Mariner OG). Unchanged, Clark came on for Withe as a substitute and scored his only ever league goal.

29th April 1978 v Birmingham City (H). 0-0. O'Hare in for McGovern, Woodcock in for Bowyer with Gemmill moving to number eight. Bowyer came on for Woodcock as a substitute.

2nd May 1978 v West Bromwich Albion (A). 2-2 (Bowyer, Robertson penalty). Lloyd in for Needham, Bowyer in for Woodcock.

4th May 1978 v Liverpool (A). 0-0. Clark in for Burns.

19th August 1978 v Tottenham H (H). 1-1 (O'Neill). Shilton, Anderson, Barrett, McGovern, Needham, Burns, O'Neill, Gemmill, Withe, Woodcock, Robertson. Peter Withe's final game.

22nd August 1978 v Coventry City (A). 0-0. Elliott in for Withe.

26th August 1978 v Queens Park Rangers (A). 0-0. Unchanged.

2nd September 1978 v West Bromwich Albion (H). 0-0. Unchanged.

9th September 1978 v Arsenal (H). 2-1 (Bowyer, Robertson penalty). Lloyd in for Needham, Mills in for O'Neill, Bowyer in for Gemmill, Birtles in for Elliott. Gary Mills' debut.

16th September 1978 v Manchester United (A). 1-1 (Bowyer). Gemmill in for Mills.

23rd September 1978 v Middlesbrough (H). 2-2 (O'Neill, Birtles). O'Neill in for Gemmill. O'Hare came on for Barrett as a substitute.

30th September 1978 v Aston Villa (A). 2-1 (Woodcock, Robertson penalty). Gemmill in for Barrett, Bowyer moved to number three.

7th October 1978 v Wolverhampton Wanderers (H). 3-0 (Birtles two, O'Neill). Clark in for Bowyer, who came on for Woodcock as a substitute.

14th October 1978 v Bristol City (A). 3-1 (Birtles, Robertson two). O'Hare in for Woodcock.

21st October 1978 v Ipswich Town (H). 1-0 (O'Neill). Bowyer in for Gemmill, Woodcock in for O'Hare.

28th October 1978 v Southampton (A). 0-0. Bowyer in for Clark, Gemmill in for O'Neill, O'Hare in for Bowyer. Needham came on for McGovern as a substitute.

4th November 1978 v Everton (H). 0-0. O'Neill in for McGovern,

O'Hare moved to number four, Gemmill moved to number seven.

11th November 1978 v Tottenham Hotspur (A). 3-1 (Anderson, Birtles, Robertson). Needham in for Burns, Mills in for O'Neill.

18th November 1978 v Queens Park Rangers (H). 0-0. Both Needham and O'Hare, and Mills and Gemmill, swapped shirt numbers.

25th November 1978 v Bolton Wanderers (A). 1-0 (Robertson). Clark in for O'Hare, O'Neill in for Mills, Bowyer moved to number six. O'Hare came on for Lloyd as a substitute.

After the Anfield loss Clough said: "I congratulated our lads on a magnificent run. This defeat means a light relief. But we would have felt better if we hadn't lost."

THE FORGOTTEN FORESTERS

The aborted 1939/40 season truncated the careers of the majority of footballers upon the outbreak of war, but for three Forest players, the deletion of that three-game season completely wiped their Reds careers from history. All three had been signed by Billy Walker during the close season, and all played all three games (lost 4-0 at Barnsley, beat Newcastle 2-0 at home and Newport County 2-1, also at home), but none of them returned when football recommenced in 1946. Andy McCall was an inside-right who had been signed from Huddersfield Town. A Scot, McCall had played for Ayr United and St Johnstone before joining the Terriers. After the war he played for Dundee, then had a disastrous spell in charge of Dundee United in 1958. Newly installed on the left wing was Jackie Maund, who had been a brief success with Aston Villa in 1936/37 before falling out of favour and joining Forest. He guested for several teams during the war before joining Walsall as a player in 1946 for two seasons. He passed away in 1993. The third player was a little-known right-winger named Colin Perry, who was also signed from Aston Villa having not played for them. Perry was born in Sheffield and joined the Villains from Gainsborough Trinity in December 1936. One source reports that Perry died during the war.

WORST TEAM EVER?

By 2007, the sinking ship SS Nottingham Forest Football Club had become accustomed to having humiliations handed out by 'lesser' teams, ones that hardly befitted the respect that two-time European Cup winners might have expected. Luton Town, Accrington Stanley, Salisbury City, Macclesfield Town and Chester City would be among those who helped Forest comes to terms with their new reality, but surely the nadir was reached on 18th October 2005, when Forest were booted out of the LDV Trophy by Football Conference side Woking, losing 3-2. Woking took the lead though Mark Rawle after ten minutes and although goals from Eugen Bopp and Spencer Weir-Daley gave Forest the lead at half-time, a second Rawle goal and one from Justin Richards eventually handed Woking a deserved victory. The guilty men who 'represented' Gary Megson's Forest that evening were as follows: Paul Gerrard, Kevin James, John Thompson, Vincent Fernandez, Martin Vickerton, Eugen Bopp (sub Jon-Paul Pittman), Gary Holt, Ross Gardner, Felix Bastians, Eugene Dadi and Spencer Weir-Daley.

A DOUBLE FIRST

On 3rd September 1892, Forest played their first game in the Football League, away at Everton. It was also the first league game played at Everton's new home ground of Goodison Park after the club had vacated its previous home of Anfield. Understandably, a capacity crowd of 14,000 were on hand to witness this double first, many of whom may have had their initial enthusiasm tempered when inside-left Horace Pike gave the new boys the lead. The game ended all-square, with Nottingham-born Fred Geary and Alf Milward scoring for Everton and "Sandy" Higgins a second for Forest. Everton were considered among the favourites for the title that term but ended the season by finishing in third place behind champions Sunderland and runners-up Preston North End, and were also beaten in that season's FA Cup Final by the unfancied Wolverhampton Wanderers. Forest themselves would finish a reasonable tenth out of 16 teams. The sides that day were as follows; Forest: Bill Brown, Martin Earp, Adam Scott, K Hamilton, Albert Smith, Peter McCracken, Neil McCallum, "Tich" Smith, "Sandy" Higgins, Horace Pike and Tom McInnes. Everton: David Jardine, Bob Howarth, James Dewar, Dickie Boyle, Johnny Holt, Hope Robertson, Alex Latta, Alan Maxwell, Fred Geary, Edgar Chadwick and Alf Milward.

TOP TEN TRANSFERS IN

These are the players who have cost Forest the most amount of money. Note that some of these fees are estimates as the actual fee in some cases was not disclosed:

1   Pierre van Hooijdonk (from Celtic, March 1997)..............£4.5m
2   David Johnson (from Ipswich Town, January 2001)..........£3.5m
3   Ricky Scimeca (from Aston Villa, July 1991).......................£3m
4   Bryan Roy (from Foggia, August 1994) £2.9m
5   Kevin Campbell (from Arsenal, July 1995) £2.8m
6   Rob Earnshaw (from Derby County, May 2008)............. £2.65m
7= Chris Bart-Williams (from Sheffield W, July 1995) £2.5m
7= Nigel Quashie (from QPR, August 1998) £2.5m
9   Andy Johnson (from Norwich City, July 1997)..................£2.2m
10= Teddy Sheringham (from Millwall, July 1991) £2m
10= Alan Rogers (from Tranmere Rovers, July 1997) £2m
10= Stan Collymore (from Southend United, July 1993) £2m

The Collymore fee rose to £2.75m once certain conditions were met.

TOP TEN TRANSFERS OUT

These are the players who have been sold by the club for the most amount of money. Again, some fees are estimates:

1   Stan Collymore (to Liverpool, July 1995).........................£8.5m
2   Steve Stone (to Aston Villa, March 1999)........................£5.5m
3   Jermaine Jenas (to Newcastle United, February 2002) £5m
4= Michael Dawson (to Tottenham Hotspur, January 2005) ...£4m
4= Andy Reid (to Tottenham Hotspur, January 2005) £4m
6   Roy Keane (to Manchester United, July 1993).............. £3.75m
7   Pierre van Hooijdonk (to Vitesse Arnhem, June 1999)....£3.5m
8= Kevin Campbell (to Trabzonspor, July 1998)....................£2.5m
8= Colin Cooper (to Middlesbrough, August 1998) £2.5m
8= David Prutton (to Southampton, January 2003)..............£2.5m

The Collymore and Keane deals were, at the time, British record transfers. Dawson and Reid moved for a combined fee of £8m.

NUMBER SIX IS...

Jack Burkitt. Before Bobby McKinlay broke all the appearance records going, Forest's leading appearance holder and owner of the title "Mr Consistency" was wing-half Burkitt, who was born in Wednesbury (like his manager at Forest, Billy Walker) on 19th January 1926. He began his football career at his local club Darlaston and soon came to the attention of many a league side, signing for Forest at the start of 1947/48. Burkitt established himself in the Forest team just as they were relegated to the Third Division South and soon became a regular in the left wing-half position as an unfussy and creative player, switching to right wing-half when necessary. Burkitt helped steer the club out of the third tier in 1951, then back to the top flight in 1957, by which time he had been appointed club captain. The pinnacle of his Forest career came in 1959 when he lifted the FA Cup at Wembley after Forest had beaten Luton Town 2-1. By this time he was reaching the veteran stage of his career, and the signing of Jim Iley and the emergence of Calvin Palmer in the early-1960s put paid to Burkitt's position as a first-choice pick. He retired in 1962, finishing with a record 463 league appearances and 14 goals. He joined the coaching staff, but was lured across the Trent in 1966 to take up the managership of Notts County. Burkitt was not a success at Meadow Lane, and was recruited as a coach at Derby County by a certain Brian Clough a year later. He left the Baseball Ground in 1969 due to ill health. It was his last role in professional football. Burkitt passed away in September 2003.

CAPTAIN JJ

While Forest can't claim the record of having the youngest-ever captain in English league football, that record belonging to Chelsea and Ray Wilkins, they have had one just a few months older. That skipper was Jermaine Jenas who, on the occasion of his final appearance at the City Ground, became Forest's youngest-ever captain, just 19 days away from his 19th birthday. Unfortunately for Jenas, a Robert Prosinecki goal seven minutes from time handed visitors Portsmouth a single goal victory and tainted the youngster's big day. Jenas' proposed £5m move to Newcastle United was completed a few days later.

THE RECORD HOLDERS #1

Most appearances – Bob McKinlay (685, 1951-69)

Surely one of the most consistent players to ever play professional football, Bob McKinlay was a steady and reliable centre-half who wore the number five shirt for the Reds for close on two decades. He was a Scot who was born in Lochgelly in Fife on 10th October 1932 and who was recommended to Forest by his uncle, Billy McKinlay, who had played for Forest for several years before the Second World War. McKinlay largely replaced the veteran Horace Gager at the centre of Forest's defence during the 1954/55 season, and never looked back. During one impressive run, McKinlay made 265 consecutive league appearances for Forest between April 1959 and October 1965, missed a single league game against Aston Villa, then played in the next consecutive 134 games, hence missing one game out of a possible 400. During that time he won an FA Cup winner's medal in 1959, played in the 'nearly' double side of 1966/67, and captained the club in Europe. The only mystery to McKinlay's career was his continual passing over by a succession of managers (including at one stage, his own in Andy Beattie) to be picked to represent Scotland. McKinlay was still playing for Forest at the age of 37, but with his place in the side taken by the emerging Liam O'Kane, he decided to retire at the end of the 1969/70 season after a stunning 614 league appearances for the Reds. When McKinlay passed away in August 2002 it was genuinely one of the saddest days in Forest's history.

FOREST'S TOP TEN APPEARANCE-MAKERS

1   Bob McKinlay ....685 (1951-1969, 611+3 league)
2   Ian Bowyer.................... 564 (1973-80, 1981-86, 425+20 league)
3   Steve Chettle ....526 (1987-2000, 398+17 league)
4   Stuart Pearce.......................................522 (1985-97, 401 league)
5   John Robertson............. 514 (1970-82, 1985-86, 381+14 league)
6   Jack Burkitt...503 (1946-61, 464 league)
7   Jack Armstrong....................................460 (1905-22, 432 league)
8   Grenville Morris...........................460 (1898-1912, 423 league)
9   Geoff Thomas ....431 (1946-60, 403 league)
10 Viv Anderson..................................430 (1974-83, 323+5 league)

MR VERSATILITY

In the olden days, several teams would have a utility player – someone who could cover several positions with equal aplomb. The most famous was Leeds United's Paul Madeley, who quite simply, could play anywhere. Forest's closest answer to Madeley was Ian Bowyer, who joined in 1973 from Orient as a winger before becoming a striker, an attacking midfielder then finally a defensive midfielder once he'd returned from a year away from the City Ground at Sunderland. Bowyer had actually burst on to the football scene as a teenage striking sensation at Manchester City before the goals had dried up and he'd been sent off to Brisbane Road. Bowyer managed to appear in every number red shirt available, including the goalkeeper's jersey (in an emergency following an injury during a game), except for number five during his time at the club. Below is a full list of each shirt and the first time Bowyer appeared in it:

1............. v Oxford United (Second Division), 20th September 1975
2................................. v West Ham (First Division), 4th March 1978
3........................ v Aston Villa (First Division), 20th September 1978
4.................................... v Norwich (First Division), 1st October 1977
5.. No appearances
6.......................................v Peterborough (FA Cup), 1st January 1976
7............................... v Brighton (League Cup), 13th December 1978
8........................... v Norwich (Second Division), 12th October 1974
9........................v Charlton (Second Division), 24th September 1975
10.................v Oxford United (Second Division), 31st August 1974
11...................... v Bristol City (Second Division), 17th August 1974
12............................ v Millwall (Second Division), 19th August 1974

In total, Bowyer accumulated 564 senior games for the club despite the year out at Sunderland and not being a regular between 1977 and 1982.

AN UNWANTED RECORD?

At the time of writing, striker Emile Sinclair holds the, perhaps, unwanted record of making the most appearances for Forest from the substitutes' bench without ever making his full first team debut. Sinclair, who was released in 2009 and joined Macclesfield Town, made 18 appearances without ever starting a game. He is a good ten games ahead of the next player in the list, Brian Cash.

THE MANAGERS

A complete list of Nottingham Forest's managers and their individual game records. Only persons to have held the official title of manager are included. For the record, Forest's list of secretary/managers is as follows: 1889-98 Harry Radford, 1897-1909 Harry Haslam, 1909-12 Fred Earp, 1912-25 Bob Masters, 1925-29 John Baynes, 1930-31 Stan Hardy and 1931-36 Noel Watson.

Harry Wightman (July 1936 – March 1939)

Forest's first manager in charge of team affairs rather than the previous post of secretarial manager, Wightman was a fairly unremarkable player with Chesterfield and Derby County (and played for Forest during the First World War) who became an unremarkable manager. He haD spells at Luton and Mansfield before taking charge at Forest, and left the Reds in March 1939 without achieving much at all. In his three seasons at the helm the club finished 18th, 20th and 20th in the second tier. Wightman passed away in 1945, aged 51.

P	W	D	L	F	A	W%	Av
114	32	26	56	151	220	0.281	1.07

Billy Walker (March 1939 – June 1960)

A legendary player at Aston Villa between the wars, ex-Sheffield Wednesday boss (he had won the FA Cup in 1935) Walker took over at Forest and remained in charge for over 20 years, in all effect becoming "Mr Nottingham Forest". He was allowed to rebuild the club from the ground up after the Second World War, and possessed a knack for spotting raw talent and getting his Reds to play good football. Despite seeing his side fall in the Third Division South in 1949, Walker was allowed to remain in charge and under his successful stewardship he brought the club from the third tier in 1951 then back to the top flight in 1957, the pinnacle of his career being the FA Cup win in 1959 at Wembley against Luton Town. Ill health forced him to relinquish the Forest hot-seat in 1960, and he sadly passed away four years later.

P	W	D	L	F	A	W%	Av
607	256	134	217	1017	863	0.422	1.49

Andy Beattie (September 1960 – June 1963)

The then Scotland manager and ex-Scotland international Beattie took over a struggling Forest side in 1960 and built upon the foundations laid down by Walker, relying on youth and passing football. After a lacklustre start he guided Forest to ninth in 1962/63, but background rumblings saw him surprisingly hand in his resignation that summer. He went on to manage Plymouth Argyle and Wolves. Beattie died in 1983, aged 70.

P	W	D	L	F	A	W%	Av
122	44	27	51	188	216	0.361	1.30

Johnny Carey (July 1963 – December 1968)

The legendary Irish international, who won the Footballer of the Year award in 1949 during a glittering career with Manchester United, took over from Beattie in the summer of 1963. He had already taken the unfashionable Leyton Orient to the top flight in 1962 and continued his success with Forest, building the finest side the City Ground had yet seen. The club were runners-up and FA Cup semi-finalists in 1966/67, but it went sour extremely quickly, not helped by the signing of Jim Baxter, and after a poor run Carey was unexpectedly sacked. He had a second spell in charge at Blackburn Rovers but was sacked in 1971 after they were relegated. Carey passed away on 23rd August 1995 at the age of 76.

P	W	D	L	F	A	W%	Av
233	87	61	85	337	351	0.373	1.38

Matt Gillies (January 1969 – October 1972)

The name that makes the more senior of Forest fans shudder. Gillies came to Forest after a successful decade at Leicester, but struggled, relegating the side in 1972. Forest spent three years being a selling club and the veterans and youngsters brought in to replace the stars that were sold weren't up to it. When it became clear that Forest weren't likely to bounce back at the first attempt, Gillies was given the boot. He died on Christmas Eve 1998, aged 77.

P	W	D	L	F	A	W%	Av
158	43	43	72	166	247	0.272	1.09

Dave Mackay (October 1972 – October 1973)

Another ex-Footballer of the Year (he shared the award with Manchester City's Tony Book in 1969), Mackay was a vastly experienced no-nonsense defensive player-turned-manager who was poached from Swindon Town in October 1973. Mackay steadied the rocky post-Gillies ship without creating major waves but just as things seemed to be starting to progress, news came through of Brian Clough and Peter Taylor's resignation at Derby. Mackay was the Derby board's choice to fill that massive chasm, and so he departed after less than a year at the City Ground. He won the title at Derby in 1975 but was sacked in November 1976. He later managed Walsall and Birmingham City, as well as several sides in the far east.

P	W	D	L	F	A	W%	Av
40	13	12	15	49	44	0.325	1.28

Allan Brown (October 1973 – January 1975)

Brown came closest of all the managers, before Brian Clough, to guiding Forest back to the top flight after their relegation in 1972. Forest flirted with promotion in the 1973/74 season, mainly thanks to the sudden blossoming of Duncan McKenzie and the purchases of George Lyall and Ian Bowyer, and reached the FA Cup quarter-final where they were unfairly dumped out of the competition by Newcastle United. McKenzie was sold in the summer of 1974 for £240,000, and Brown did not spend the money well. With Forest drifting towards the bottom of the table, Brown was sacked after a 2-0 home defeat by Notts County. He went on to take charge at Blackpool and Southport. Brown passed away on 20th April 2011 at the age of 84.

P	W	D	L	F	A	W%	Av
50	17	15	18	59	62	0.340	1.32

Brian Clough (January 1975 – May 1993)

For more on Brian Clough, see elsewhere – in fact most of the rest of this volume.

P	W	D	L	F	A	W%	Av
759	331	208	220	1124	837	0.436	1.58

Frank Clark (May 1993 – December 1996)

Brian Clough's choice to succeed him as boss was his old left-back, and it was a surprising one as Clark had barely achieved a thing in nine years at Leyton Orient, and had recently moved into the boardroom. Clark splashed out where Clough had been reluctant and guided the Reds back into the top flight after just one term, then to a magnificent third-placed finish in the Premiership and Uefa Cup football. Things turned sour for Clark towards the end of 1996, and with Forest at the foot of the table, he resigned. He returned as chairman in 2011.

P	W	D	L	F	A	W%	Av
143	61	45	37	210	175	0.427	1.59

Dave Bassett (March 1997 (joint) – January 1999)

Brought in to aid Stuart Pearce who was acting as caretaker player/manager following the resignation of Frank Clark, then succeeded him when Psycho left. Bassett had been the brains behind the remarkable rise of Wimbledon to the top flight, and had also managed Crystal Palace, Watford and Sheffield United. Bassett got Forest promoted in 1997/98 but the club were soon struggling back in the Premiership, mainly thanks to the sales of forward Kevin Campbell and captain and terrace hero Colin Cooper, plus the strike of Pierre van Hooijdonk. Sacked in January 1999 with Forest's threadbare squad bottom of the Premiership and dumped out of the FA Cup by Portsmouth.

P	W	D	L	F	A	W%	Av
67	30	17	20	100	83	0.448	1.60

Ron Atkinson (January – May 1999)

A time Forest fans tend to pretend didn't happen. "Big Ron" cemented Forest's relegation, brought in loads of lacklustre players and masterminded Forest's home 'nine-goal thriller' when they lost 8-1 to Manchester United at the City Ground. Retired from management in May 1999.

P	W	D	L	F	A	W%	Av
17	5	2	10	17	29	0.294	1.00

David Platt (July 1999 – July 2001)

The hugely ambitious ex-England captain was brought in with no managerial experience beside an aborted stint at Sampdoria, and given the pen to benefactor Nigel Doughty's chequebook. Platt's ambition never matched his managerial talents despite spending millions on the likes of Ricky Scimeca, Salvatore Matrecano, Gianluca Petrachi and David Johnson, and he jumped ship in July 2001 to take charge of the England under-21 team. Forest have never quite recovered from Platt's time in charge, particularly financially. After a spell out of football, Platt was called in by Roberto Mancini at Manchester City, and was first team coach when they won the Premiership in 2011/12.

P	W	D	L	F	A	W%	Av
92	34	22	36	108	109	0.370	1.35

Paul Hart (July 2001 – February 2004)

Hart was the massively popular manager of the Forest Academy who Doughty saw as the man to get the Reds back into the top flight without requiring the funds lavished on David Platt, and it so nearly worked as Hart's team of cherubic talents just failed in the 2003 play-offs. That team largely collapsed in the summer of that year, and in February 2004, after 14 league games without a win, Hart was shown the door.

P	W	D	L	F	A	W%	Av
121	39	40	42	166	139	0.405	1.55

Joe Kinnear (February – December 2004)

A man with bags of experience as a player with Tottenham Hotspur and Brighton as well as a manager at Wimbledon and Luton Town, Kinnear was recruited to somehow save Forest from drowning in the 2003/04 season, and he achieved it, lifting the Reds to a miraculous mid-table finish with "sexy football". The next season was awful though, and Kinnear resigned after losing 3-0 at Derby County.

P	W	D	L	F	A	W%	Av
40	12	15	13	49	54	0.300	1.28

Gary Megson (January 2005 – February 2006)

Possibly, with the exception of "Big Ron", Forest's most unpopular manager ever. A brief but invisible ex-Red, Megson couldn't prevent the slide of the club into the third tier for the first time since 1951, but then couldn't seem to do much right once in League 1 as the slow demise of NFFC seemed to be accelerating. Megson had had a nomadic but successful playing career with Plymouth, Everton, Sheffield Wednesday, Forest (although he later admitted he spent most of his time at the City Ground hiding from Brian Clough), Newcastle United, Manchester City, Norwich City, Shrewsbury Town and Lincoln City, and had managed West Bromwich Albion into the top flight twice. Megson resigned in February 2006 with barely a single fan among the entirety of the Forest support, and was replaced by a caretaker duo of Frank Barlow and Ian McParland who performed heroics in grinding the Reds back up the table and just a toe away from the play-offs.

P	W	D	L	F	A	W%	Av
51	15	16	20	55	64	0.294	1.20

Colin Calderwood (May 2006 – December 2008)

Another brief ex-Red, Calderwood was brought in from Northampton Town with a decent reputation, and within six months Forest were strides ahead in League 1. Calderwood had been a successful top flight defender mainly with Tottenham Hotspur and had won 41 caps for Scotland during his playing days before taking over at Northampton Town and guiding them to automatic promotion to League 1 in 2006. Calderwood chose Forest over Ipswich Town and despite his good start Forest couldn't hold on to the lead they had established and they just scraped into the play-offs where they lost to Yeovil in embarrassing fashion. Losing 2-0 from the first leg at Huish Park, the Glovers hammered Forest 5-2 at the City Ground. The following year it looked like the play-offs again until an end-of-season spurt ended Forest's League 1 nightmare with automatic promotion. The higher sphere proved too much for Calderwood and he was sacked as Forest struggled in the Championship.

P	W	D	L	F	A	W%	Av
117	49	38	30	152	109	0.419	1.58

Billy Davies (January 2009 – June 2011)

A former Derby County boss, Davies initially secured Forest's survival in the Championship then, with some astute transfer dealings, assembled the best Forest side seen at the City Ground for almost a decade. Davies had had a very unremarkable playing career with Rangers, Elfsborg in Sweden, St Mirren, Leicester City and Motherwell. He'd managed Motherwell, Preston (who he nearly guided into the top flight in 2005 and 2006) then at Pride Park oversaw Derby's rise to the Premiership in 2007 via a play-off win over West Bromwich Albion. He lasted until November before being sacked by Derby, who were bottom of the top flight at the time. Davies, despite his constant grumblings with the Forest board's seemingly penny-pinching transfer acquisition panel, guided the Reds to two successive play-off appearances, although they failed in both of them. It was still a surprise though when Davies was sacked by Nigel Doughty in June 2011.

P	W	D	L	F	A	W%	Av
112	50	33	29	158	117	0.446	1.63

Steve McClaren (June – October 2011)

See The Wally with the Brolly on page 56.

P	W	D	L	F	A	W%	Av
10	2	2	6	10	21	0.200	0.800

Steve Cotterill (October 2011 onwards)

Not the most popular appointment ever, the ex-Notts County boss was prised from fellow Championship strugglers Portsmouth to replace Steve McClaren. The momentum from a quiet start swiftly evaporated and most fans resigned themselves to another slide into the third tier after a spell in which Forest just could not score. But, with the loan signing of Adlène Guedioura, the resurgence of Andy Reid, the emergence of Garath McCleary and the recovery of Dexter Blackstock, Cotterill unexpectedly guided the Reds out of danger and secured their Championship place.

P	W	D	L	F	A	W%	Av
35	12	6	17	38	41	0.343	1.26

THE LOCAL TEAM FOR LOCAL PEOPLE XI

A team made up of players who played for Nottingham Forest and were born within a Johnny Metgod free-kick of the City Ground:

1 Peter Wells...(born Nottingham)
2 Viv Anderson.................................. (born Clifton, Nottingham)
3 Julian Bennett....................... (born The Meadows, Nottingham)
4 Chris Fairclough...(born Nottingham)
5 Steve Chettle ....(born Nottingham)
6 Henry Newton ....(born Nottingham)
7 Jermaine Jenas..(born Nottingham)
8 Steve Hodge ....(born Gedling, Nottingham)
9 Garry Birtles...(born Nottingham)
10 Andrew Cole..(born Nottingham)
11 Darren Huckerby...(born Nottingham)

Other locally-born players include the long-serving Bill Morley, defensive stalwarts Wes Morgan and Kelvin Wilson and sepia-tinted legends such as Tinsley Lindley and John Sands.

STRIKE!

The summer of 1998 should have been a good one to be a Forest fan. Back in the Premiership after one season out, any Reds supporter should have been salivating with anticipation at the thought of the lethal Campbell–van Hooijdonk strike partnership chewing away at opposition defences, backed by flying winger Steve Stone, rock-solid captain Colin Cooper and potential new boy Wim Jonk, the Dutch international. But it didn't happen. Kevin Campbell was sold to Turkish side Trabzonspor before the season commenced, and just a few games in Cooper was unexpectedly sold to Middlesbrough. Jonk then joined Sheffield Wednesday. As for Pierre van Hooijdonk, he famously accused the club of a lack of ambition and reneging on a deal to allow him to leave once promotion had been achieved in 1998, and refused to return to the side from his native Holland. The strike lasted four months but by the time van Hooijdonk returned the damage was permanent. He was allegedly ostracised by his team-mates and only scored six goals in the comically-struggling Forest side that season before being sold to Vitesse Arnhem for £3.5m the following summer.

CLIFTON-BORN FORMER FOREST STAR VIV ANDERSON

NUMBER SEVEN IS...

Duncan McKenzie. The period between 1968 and 1975 was not a happy time to be a Forest fan. The 1966/67 season had promised much, with a runners-up spot in the league and an FA Cup semi-final spot. But what followed was a routine dismantling of the side, with heroes such as Henry Newton, Terry Hennessey and Ian Storey-Moore being sold and replaced with doughty veterans like Tommy Jackson, Doug Fraser and Tommy Gemmell. But there was one spark of joy that Forest fans could count on (although not all the time), and that was Duncan McKenzie. Signed from school in July 1968, McKenzie was a young man of 17 upon making his first team debut 14 months later. His early career seemed mainly hit-and-miss (including two loan spells at Mansfield Town), but he had eventually established himself in the Forest team by 1972 and his skills, flair, trickery and cheeky arrogance became a rare highlight of the Reds' play. The 1973/74 season was easily McKenzie's best, scoring 28 goals in all competitions and leading Forest's charge in the FA Cup that was unfairly curtailed by Newcastle's hooligans and the incompetence of the FA. He was also called into the England squad by Sir Alf Ramsey in April 1974 for a friendly in Portugal, but failed to make the team. McKenzie's prowess attracted the attention of bigger teams and after he turned down the option of a new contract with Forest he was transferred to Brian Clough's Leeds United in the summer for £240,000. From that point on McKenzie never seemed to quite fulfil his tremendous potential, embarking on a nomadic career that saw him spend brief spells at Anderlecht, Everton, Chelsea and Blackburn Rovers then Tulsa and Chicago in the US. His career petered out at the tender age of 31. He later worked in media and as an after-dinner speaker.

GOOD TO BE BACK...NOT!

In May 1979, the all-conquering Nottingham Forest journeyed to Munich's Olympic Stadium and beat Malmö to win the European Cup. Their next trip to the same stadium, a mere two months later, could not have been more different. Despite the presence of new signings Frank Gray and Asa Hartford, a full-strength Forest went down 5-0 against Bayern Munich in a pre-season friendly.

IN THE PINK

For a match at home to Barnsley in September 1932 the local press reported Forest had been presented with a brand new kit of Viyella (a blend of wool and cotton) shirts by Sir Ernest Jardine, the Alan Sugar of the 1930s (in Nottingham's lace industry anyhow). All well and good, except that the shirts were salmon pink in colour. It is not known how long the shirts lasted.

FORTRESS CITY GROUND

When Brighton and Hove Albion, bottom of the First Division, beat Forest 1-0 at the City Ground on 17th November 1979, it ended the club's record run of 51 games unbeaten at home. The last team to have beaten Forest at the City Ground were Cardiff City on 23rd April 1977 in the Second Division, a remarkable period of almost two and a half years, encompassing the entire 1977/78 and 1978/79 seasons. The fact that Brighton were such lowly opposition at the time was hard enough to bear, but to add extra pain to the defeat, Forest had been awarded a penalty, but the Seagulls' Graham Moseley saved John Robertson's spot kick.

LIKE FATHER, LIKE SONS

For a father to have his son follow in his footsteps as a professional footballer is hardly a rarity, but one Forest player had the privilege of seeing no less than four sons make it in varying degrees. He is George Wilkins, who the Reds signed from Bradford Park Avenue for £7,500 in December 1947. An inside-right, Wilkins scored on his debut and went on to find the net six times in 24 league games before joining Leeds United in September 1949. As for his sons, the most famous by far is Ray Wilkins, who enjoyed a fantastic career at Chelsea, Manchester United and Queens Park Rangers to name but three of his 11 clubs, as well as winning 84 caps for England. Son number two, Graham, spent a decade at Chelsea and two years at Brentford, while youngest son Dean made over 350 appearances for Brighton and Hove Albion and managed them between 2006 and 2008. The final brother was Steve, a professional at both Chelsea and Brentford but who failed to make a league appearance for either.

YOU'RE OFF!

When George Pritty was sent off for Forest against Millwall on 25th March 1939, it was to be another 30 years before another Forest player was dismissed, this dubious honour falling to Sammy Chapman, on 27th November 1971 at Leeds United for felling Mick Jones with a punch. This fact would be remarkable if not that most other clubs could boast similar records during this time in footballing history, when players could even in some cases attempt murder without fear of an early bath. After Pritty, the next player to be sent off in a game involving Forest was Viggo Jenson, for Hull City in April 1952, then it was the turn of Aston Villa's Derek Dougan, dismissed in September 1962 for apparently arguing with the referee for 36 minutes. Future Forest flop Jim Baxter was sent off in December 1965 while playing for Sunderland for punching Sammy Chapman, while Billy Bremner (Leeds United, January 1967) and Mick Doyle (Manchester City, May 1967) were both dismissed for bad fouls on Forest's outside-right Barry Lyons. As football moved into the 1970s, referees suddenly found themselves pointing to the tunnel with a deal more zealousness and Neil Martin (for Forest v Preston, September 1973, arguing with the referee), Frank Saul (for Millwall v Forest, October 1973, fighting), Liam O'Kane (for Forest v Middlesbrough, December 1973, two bookings – the second later rescinded) all received their marching orders. Tommy Jackson was sent off for Forest in February 1974 for fighting with Orient's Ricky Heppolette (who was also dismissed), then Pat Howard of Newcastle went for persistent arguing during the infamous 1974 FA Cup quarter-final at St James' Park. Chapman completed a hat-trick of dismissals in October 1974 (v Norwich) and October 1975 (at Fulham), sandwiching David Jones' sending-off at Orient in November 1974. Of course, in 1975 Brian Clough took charge and put an end to all this nonsense, and no Forest player saw red until August 1980 when Martin O'Neill was dismissed for fighting with Birmingham City's Mark Dennis. More than 80 Forest players have been sent off since that date, with the record number of dismissals being held by David Prutton, with four. Incidentally, the first recorded dismissal for Forest was Enoch "Knocker" West, who was sent off on 13th March 1909 in a FA Cup tie with Derby County. The only other players to be dismissed between then and Pritty's dismissal were Fred Parker in January 1922 and Percy Barratt in September 1928.

WEMBLEY WOE

Forest's record League Cup run between 1976 and 1980 finally came to an end in March 1980 and at possibly the worst place imaginable – Wembley Stadium. Having reached the final for an unprecedented third season running, Forest faltered at the last step, losing 1-0 to Wolverhampton Wanderers, and to a goal mostly of their own making. A lumped ball by Peter Daniel should have posed no problems for David Needham and Peter Shilton, but Needham chose to chest the ball past Shilton then comically run into him, leaving Andy Gray free to nip past them for a simple tap-in. To make it just a little worse, Wolves were managed by ex-Reds midfield maestro John Barnwell, and captained by Emlyn Hughes who had been the losing captain in the 1978 final between Forest and Liverpool. Wolves therefore became the first side to beat Forest in the League Cup since Coventry City way back in September 1976 when the Reds were still a Second Division side.

AND I AM UNANIMOUS IN THAT

An article in the 1960 Forest programme against Fulham expressed vehement opposition to a proposed rule change. "Nothing in sport all over the world has been open to abuse and has, in fact, been abused quite so often," said the report. "The Football Association have seen it abused, and so have Football League clubs and the general public, who will have the last say if the game is handed over to the 'three-card trickster' minds." The mooted change that spawned such ire? The use of substitutes.

LAST MAN STANDING (1898)

In the first Forest programme of 1962/63 there came the sad news that Alf Spouncer, the last surviving member of the 1898 FA Cup-winning team, had passed away at his home at Southend-on-Sea, leaving a widow, three sons and a daughter. Alf, who reached the age of 85, played outside-left in Forest's first FA Cup win at Crystal Palace against Derby and had joined from Gainsborough where his father was a chemist. He played for the Reds for a magnificent 12 seasons, and gained a single England cap. After football he joined the flour business in London and served in the First World War in the Black Watch.

LOS GALACTICOS

Perhaps an obscure pub quiz question one might hear is: "Which Englishman led Real Madrid to their second La Liga title in 1933?" The obscure answer is Robert Firth. What is even more obscure is that he was a former Forest player, turning out on the right wing for three seasons just before the First World War. Firth later played for Port Vale and Southend United before moving to Spain and ending up as head coach of Racing de Santander, leading them to the runners-up spot in La Liga in 1931. He replaced Lippo Hertza at Real Madrid in 1932 and guided his new charges to the title. Unfortunately he couldn't repeat this achievement a year later and departed. Firth's success was the last La Liga title Madrid would win for two decades.

BARGAIN BUYS #1

£47,000 is perhaps quite a sum to risk on a fresh-faced 18-year-old with no league experience on the evidence of a brief trial, but when that player goes on to serve magnificently for three seasons before being sold for a British record £3.75m, such a fee could only be described as money well spent. The player in question was Roy Maurice Keane, who matured from that fresh-faced youngster into one of the greatest British midfielders of his generation. After being turned down by a succession of clubs in Ireland and England, Cork-born Keane turned out for semi-professional side Cobh Ramblers while taking on a succession of manual employment jobs. Keane's big break came in the summer of 1990 when he was spotted by Forest's Irish scout Noel McCabe in an FAI Youth Cup match. McCabe invited Keane to Nottingham for a trial and the youngster impressed Brian Clough and his staff as a box-to-box midfielder. Keane came from nowhere to be handed a debut at Liverpool in the 1990/91 season, and never looked back. The only setback he suffered was when Clough punched him for a bad back-pass that almost led to Forest being knocked out of the FA Cup. "I couldn't have punched him very hard," mused Clough. "He got up again." Keane remained at Forest until Alex Ferguson snatched him from the grasp of Blackburn Rovers. Keane spent over a decade as Manchester United's engine room before calling time on his playing career in 2006 after a brief spell with boyhood heroes Celtic.

FOREST'S MOST CAPPED PLAYER

The holders of the title of Forest's most capped international player have been as follows:

Arthur Goodyer (England, one cap)

Forest's first capped player, he played for England against Scotland on 5th April 1879 at the Kennington Oval, London. His one cap record was equalled by Sam Widdowson, Edwin Luntley and John Sands, until it was beaten by...

Edwin Luntley (England, two caps)

Two caps in the space of three days, on March 13th and 15th 1880, both against Scotland. These were the only caps that Luntley won, and his total was bettered by...

Tinsley Lindley (England, four caps)

Lindley set a new record on 5th April, 1890 against Scotland, then won a further cap a year later against Ireland. The new record stood for almost a decade until...

Frank Forman (nine caps)

The first Forest player to captain his country, Forman broke the record with his fifth cap on 8th April 1899 against Scotland. He would go on to win a further four caps. The next record-breaker was the first non-English player to hold the record...

Grenville Morris (16 caps)

Forest's eventual record goalscorer won his tenth cap on 5th March 1910 against Scotland at Kilmarnock. He would add a further six caps to his total, and his standing as Forest's most capped player would stand for 62 years, until...

Liam O'Kane (Northern Ireland, 20 caps)

The centre-back or right-back won his 17th cap on 4th September 1974 against Norway in Oslo. He would have won many more if injury had not hampered and then curtailed his career. His record stood for almost three years until...

Martin O'Neill (Northern Ireland, 36 caps)

O'Neill celebrated Forest's promotion back to the top flight by breaking his fellow Ulsterman's record on 1st June 1977 against Scotland in Glasgow. O'Neill left Forest in 1980, after setting the new record of 36 caps, which was eventually bettered by...

Stuart Pearce (England, 76 caps)

"Psycho" regained the record for England on 25th May 1991 at Wembley against Argentina. Pearce, the 999th player to be capped for England, set the new bar at 76 with his last cap for the club against Italy on 4th June 1997.

FOREST'S MOST CAPPED PLAYERS...

1	Stuart Pearce (England)	76 (of 78)	1987-1997
2	Des Walker (England)	48 (of 59)	1988-1992
3	Martin O'Neill (Northern Ireland)	36 (of 64)	1972-1990
4	John Robertson (Scotland)	26 (of 28)	1978-1982
5	Stern John (Trinidad & Tobago)	25 (of 113)	1999-2002
6	Jim Brennan (Canada)	24 (of 49)	2000-2003
7=	Lars Bohinen (Norway)	23 (of 49)	1993-1995
7=	Alf-Inge Håland (Norway)	23 (of 34)	1994-1997
9=	Liam O'Kane (Northern Ireland)	20 (of 20)	1970-1975
9=	Toddy Örlygsson (Iceland)	20 (of 41)	1990-1993

...AND TOP INTERNATIONAL GOALSCORERS

1	Stern John (Trinidad & Tobago)	12 (of 70)	1999-2002
2	Junior Agogo (Ghana)	9 (of 12)	2006-2008
3	Grenville Morris (Wales)	8 (of 9)	1899-1912
4	John Robertson (Scotland)	7 (of 8)	1978-1982
5=	Dean Saunders (Wales)	5 (of 22)	1996-1997
5=	Stuart Pearce (England)	5 (of 5)	1987-1997
5=	Martin O'Neill (Northern Ireland)	5 (of 8)	1972-1990
8	Lars Bohinen (Norway)	4 (of 10)	1993-1995

Bryan Roy, Pierre van Hooijdonk (both Holland), Fred Forman, Trevor Francis, Tinsley Lindley, Neil Webb (all England), Rob Earnshaw (Wales), Archie Gemmill (Scotland) and Toddy Örlygsson (Iceland) all scored three.

EUROPEAN CUP-WINNING SCORERS

Forest have had five players on their books who have also scored in European Cup or Champions League finals. These are Tommy Gemmell (twice for Celtic in 1967 and 1970), Trevor Francis (for Forest in 1979), John Robertson (for Forest in 1980), Peter Withe (for Aston Villa in 1982) and Teddy Sheringham (for Manchester United in 1999).

WHY ARSENAL WEAR RED

In 1856, Frederick William Beardsley was born in Nottingham. One of Forest's earliest goalkeepers, Beardsley was sacked from his job in a government munitions factory for taking time off without permission to play in the 1884 FA Cup semi-final replay against Queen's Park at Merchiston Castle in Edinburgh. Beardsley moved to London and started work at the Royal Arsenal in Woolwich, where he was soon joined by Morris Bates, a former Forest team-mate. The pair of them helped form Dial Square, a team for Royal Arsenal employees wishing to play football. Beardsley continued to turn out for Forest and in one trip back up to his birthplace, managed to obtain a kit of Forest shirts, which were, of course, red. Dial Square began to play in this kit, and changed their name to Royal Arsenal in 1887 and then Woolwich Arsenal in 1893, before becoming plain Arsenal in 1914. The club has worn red ever since, with legendary manager Herbert Chapman adding the distinctive white sleeves in 1934.

NO SUBSTITUTE

The FA first allowed substitutes (for injured players only) at the start of the 1965/66 season, but Forest's first substitute in senior football had already happened, in 1959, when Peter Knight came on for Tommy Wilson in the FA Charity Shield against Wolves at Molineux. Forest's first league substitute was Barry McArthur, who replaced Colin Addison in the game against Leeds on 4th September, 1965. Just over a month later, David Wilson became Forest's first ever goalscoring substitute when he netted the fifth goal in a 5-0 home demolition of West Ham United, having replaced the fourth scorer, Alan Hinton. On 6th February, 1999, Manchester United's Ole Gunnar Solskjær came on with 18 minutes to go against Forest and set a new substitute goal-scoring record with four.

OLD BIG 'ED

No volume on Nottingham Forest would be complete without an extended reference to the unique genius who took the club to the dizzying heights that had not been seen before and seem to be extremely unlikely to be seen again. That man, of course, is Brian Howard Clough, who exploded into the City Ground in January 1975 and set about transforming a lacklustre provincial side with nothing but two FA Cup wins to its name into reigning European champions. Born in Middlesbrough, on 21st March 1935, Clough was the sixth of nine children. He left school with no qualifications and began work at ICI, playing football for Billingham Synthonia. After completing his national service in 1955, he joined Middlesbrough and soon made a name for himself as a prolific striker in the second tier before joining Sunderland. On Boxing Day 1962 Clough suffered a knee injury in a collision with the Bury keeper that ended his career prematurely. After taking charge of Sunderland's youth team he and his best friend Peter Taylor took the helm at Hartlepools United. The pair moved to Derby County and transformed the Rams into the best team in the country, winning the title in 1971/72. Both men resigned in October 1973 after an infamous series of disputes with the Derby board. After a brief spell at Brighton, Clough (without Taylor) took on more than he could bargain for at Leeds United, where he lasted 44 days as manager. Forest took the chance on Clough nearly four months later and he set about building a side with a mix of experience and rawness, something that came to fruition after Taylor returned as his number two in July 1976. The club won promotion back to the top flight in 1977 after a five-year absence and enjoyed three seasons of incredible success, with the league title and two European Cup wins. Clough struggled for a while when Taylor quit in 1982, but turned Forest back into a decent team, culminating in a unsuccessful FA Cup Final appearance in 1991. Clough's battle with alcohol became a losing one shortly afterwards, and in 1993, after Forest had finished bottom of the new Premiership, he resigned. Clough suffered from poor health after his retirement, mainly due to liver damage, but a transplant in 2003 seem to restore him back to his former feistiness. Sadly, on 20th September 2004, it was announced that Brian had died of stomach cancer, and the football world had lost one of its greatest ever characters.

CLOUGHIE QUOTES

"I wouldn't say I was the best manager in the business. But I was in the top one."

"If God had wanted us to play football in the clouds, he'd have put grass up there."

"If I had an argument with a player we would sit down for 20 minutes, talk about it and then decide I was right."

"I'm sure the England selectors thought if they took me on and gave me the job, I'd want to run the show. They were shrewd because that's exactly what I would have done."

"If a chairman sacks the manager he initially appointed, he should go as well."

"Don't send me flowers when I'm dead. If you like me, send them while I'm alive."

"I want no epitaphs of profound history and all that type of thing. I contributed. I would hope they would say that, and I would hope somebody liked me."

"Walk on water? I know most people out there will be saying that instead of walking on it, I should have taken more of it with my drinks. They are absolutely right."

"Players lose you games, not tactics. There's so much crap talked about tactics by people who barely know how to win at dominoes."

"I've missed him. He used to make me laugh. He was the best diffuser of a situation I have ever known. I hope he's alright." On the late Peter Taylor.

BC: "Oi? Who are you?"
Recent signing David Currie: "David Currie. You signed me from Barnsley."
BC: "I signed you? You're crap!"

ODDLY SHAPED BALLS

Forest fans were shocked to hear in April 2002 than the City Ground was to host that season's European Cup semi-final. What was even more shocking was the information it was the Heineken Cup semi-final, European rugby's premier competition, between two of the code's more exotic teams, Leicester Tigers and Llanelli. A crowd of 29,849 witnessed Leicester's thrilling 13-12 victory.

SHOOT!

In March 2002 a Forest match was abandoned after two of the Reds players were shot. Fortunately, the shots were from an air rifle, but alarmingly the match in question was an under-14s game against Sheffield Wednesday. The injured players, goalkeeper Darren Smith and right-back James Cullingworth, were said to be "shaken".

OH NO, NOT HIM AGAIN

Several players throughout history seemed to have enjoyed playing against Forest, but perhaps none more so than sharp-shooter-turned-pundit Jimmy Greaves. Greaves scored no less than 24 times against Forest in just over a decade, including three hat-tricks and two four-goal hauls. It took the Reds all this time to learn how to subdue the lethal striker, as in the two games Greaves played against Forest while at West Ham United for the 1970/71 season he failed to find the net.

15th Apr 1956.................................one for Chelsea at the City Ground
27th Sep 1958 ....three for Chelsea at Stamford Bridge
16th Apr 1960.................................one for Chelsea at Stamford Bridge
29th Apr 1961...........four (one penalty) for Chelsea at Stamford Bridge
29th Sep 1962 ....four for Tottenham Hotspur at White Hart Lane
31st Aug 1963 ....three Tottenham Hotspur at White Hart Lane
21st Dec 1963 ....one for Tottenham Hotspur at White Hart Lane
28th Dec 1964 ....one for Tottenham Hotspur at White Hart Lane
4th Feb 1967 ....one for Tottenham Hotspur at White Hart Lane
29th Apr 1967..(FAC SF) one for Tottenham Hotspur at Hillsborough
25th Oct 1967............one for Tottenham Hotspur at White Hart Lane
21st Sep 1968.............one for Tottenham Hotspur at White Hart Lane
12th Apr 1969..............one for Tottenham Hotspur at the City Ground
8th Nov 1969 ....one for Tottenham Hotspur at the City Ground

THE CURSE OF UNITED

Of all the possible transfer trails, the one it seemed, for a long time at least, to be the least likely to succeed, was the one that led players from Forest to Manchester United. The curse began with Ian Storey-Moore who left for Old Trafford in 1972. Moore performed well, initially, and became a rare bright spark in a dwindling United team shorn of its Best–Charlton–Law axis, but then suffered a serious injury that ended his top flight career after just 39 league games for United. In a slight buck to the trend veteran midfielder Tommy Jackson joined United from Forest in 1974, mainly to help with the reserve side, but impressed enough to be given around 20 appearances in the first team as a resurgent United finished third in the top flight a year after promotion. In 1980 the hottest striking property in football was Forest's Garry Birtles, who was eventually sold to United for £1.25m in October of that year. In his first season at Old Trafford Birtles failed to find the net once, and despite scoring 11 goals in his second season fell out of first team contention, returning to the City Ground in 1982. The next to chance his feet in Manchester was Peter Davenport, who left Forest in 1986. Davenport, signed as a replacement for Barcelona-bound Mark Hughes, couldn't initially replicate his Forest form in an underachieving United side, but despite finishing as leading scorer in 1986/87 was sold to Middlesbrough in 1988 following the return of Hughes. In 1989, with Forest on the cusp of greatness, one of the most crucial pieces of the side, midfielder Neil Webb, was lured by the call of United. After only a few games for the Old Trafford side Webb snapped his Achilles tendon while playing for England against Sweden and was never the same player. He rejoined Forest in 1992 for half his original transfer fee. The "curse" was finally lifted in 1993 with the record-breaking sale of Roy Keane to United.

PLAY YOUR CARDS RIGHT

While red and yellow cards are a common sight at most games these days, it is worth remembering that they were introduced as relatively recently as 1976. For the record, the first yellow card seen at the City Ground was flashed at Sheffield United left-back Paul Garner on 9th October 1976.

FOREST'S LEADING GOALSCORERS

Season-by-season, league goals only. * New club record for league goals in a single season.

1892/93	A Higgins 12*
1893/94	T McInnes 14
1894/95	A Carnelly 16*
1895/96	T McInnes 10
1896/97	C Richards 8
1897/98	L Benbow 10
1898/99	F Spencer 9
1899/00	J Calvey 16
1900/01	AG Morris 14
1901/02	J Calvey 12
1902/03	AG Morris 24*
1903/04	H Sugden 13
1904/05	W Shearman 13
1905/06	AG Morris 20
1906/07	AG Morris 21
1907/08	E West 28*
1908/09	E West 22
1909/10	AG Morris 19
1910/11	AG Morris 11
1911/12	AG Morris 10
1912/13	T Gibson 17
1913/14	J Derrick 8
1914/15	J Coleman 14
1919/20	J Lythgoe 12
1920/21	J Spaven 11
1921/22	J Spaven 18
1922/23	J Spaven 10
1923/24	D Walker 17
1924/25	D Walker 7
1925/26	S Gibson 10
1926/27	S Gibson 17
1927/28	N Burton 15
1928/29	S Jennings 15
1929/30	J Dent 15

1930/31...J Dent 23
1931/32..............................W Dickinson 21
1932/33..............................W Dickinson 14
1933/34...J Dent 27
1934/35.....................................T Peacock 21
1935/36.....................................T Peacock 20
1936/37.....................................D Martin 29*
1937/38......................................D Martin 12
1938/39.................J Surtees, H Crawshaw 9
1946/47......................................RAJ Brown 16
1947/48.....................................T Johnston 12
1948/49... G Lee 10
1949/50....................................W Ardron 25
1950/51................................. W Ardron 36*
1951/52....................................W Ardron 29
1952/53....................................W Ardron 21
1953/54.......................................A Moore 19
1954/55.................................. H McLaren 9
1955/56.......................................J Barrett 17
1956/57.......................................J Barrett 27
1957/58.......................................T Wilson 19
1958/59.......................................T Wilson 21
1959/60.......................................T Wilson 11
1960/61..C Booth 19
1961/62..C Booth 12
1962/63.....................................C Addison 16
1963/64..................................... F Wignall 16
1964/65.................C Addison, F Wignall 14
1965/66..................................... C Addison 9
1966/67........................... I Storey-Moore 21
1967/68..J Baker 16
1968/69........................... I Storey-Moore 17
1969/70........................... I Storey-Moore 11
1970/71........................... I Storey-Moore 18
1971/72........................... I Storey-Moore 13
1972/73.....................N Martin, M O'Neill,
.... D McKenzie, J Galley 6
1973/74...............................D McKenzie 26

1974/75.....................................N Martin 10
1975/76..I Bowyer 13
1976/77..P Withe 16
1977/78.................J Robertson, P Withe 12
1978/79.......................................G Birtles 14
1979/80...................................... T Francis 14
1980/81..I Wallace 11
1981/82..I Wallace 9
1982/83..I Wallace 13
1983/84...............G Birtles, P Davenport 15
1984/85............................... P Davenport 16
1985/86...................................... N Clough 15
1986/87... G Birtles, N Clough, N Webb 14
1987/88................................... N Clough 19
1988/89................................... N Clough 14
1989/90...................................... S Hodge 10
1990/91...................................... N Clough 14
1991/92............................T Sheringham 13
1992/93................................... N Clough 10
1993/94.................................. S Collymore 19
1994/95.................................. S Collymore 22
1995/96....................J Lee, B Roy, I Woan 8
1996/97................ K Campbell, A Håland 6
1997/98........................ P van Hooijdonk 29
1998/99.................................. D Freedman 9
1999/00................ D Freedman, A Rogers 9
2000/01.........................C Bart-Williams 14
2001/02...S John 13
2002/03................................... D Johnson 25
2003/04.. A Reid 13
2004/05.. G Taylor 7
2005/06..N Tyson 10
2006/07..G Holt 13
2007/08......................................M Agogo 13
2008/09................................R Earnshaw 12
2009/10................................R Earnshaw 15
2010/11.............................. L McGugan 13
2011/12................................. G McCleary 9

CROWD 4 FOREST 3

Forest have been involved in many famous matches during their time, but perhaps the most infamous one, aside from the tragedy at Hillsborough in 1989, would be the 1974 FA Cup quarter-final at St James' Park between the Reds and Newcastle United on 9th March. The Magpies were in the top flight but were on a poor run of form, whereas a young Forest side possessing the threats of George Lyall, Ian Bowyer and above all, Duncan McKenzie, were seemingly firing on all cylinders, especially after beating Manchester City 4-1 in the fifth round. Forest were soon enjoying themselves and already eyeing a semi-final place after goals from Bowyer, Liam O'Kane and a Lyall penalty had put them 3-1 up. Even better for the Reds, Newcastle defender Pat Howard had been sent off for protesting too much to the referee after the penalty award. So, two goals up and a man extra, what could possibly go wrong? How about a couple of hundred Newcastle fans streaming on to the pitch from the Leazes End in an attempt to get the match abandoned? The referee got the players off the field, but not before Forest centre-half Dave Serella was punched by a supporter. A shell-shocked Reds team later returned and were understandably below their best as ten-man Newcastle pulled it back to 3-3. Then, in the last minute, Bobby Moncur netted from an offside position (it was reported the linesman was "too scared" to raise his flag) to send Newcastle through – or so they thought. Forest protested that the crowd had unfairly influenced the outcome of the game and demanded the FA kick United out of the competition. Newcastle legend Malcolm Macdonald rightly predicted the FA would come up with a ridiculous solution and they did – the tie was declared void and it was ordered to be replayed at a neutral venue, Goodison Park. Forest battled to a 0-0 draw and looked forward to the replay at the City Ground – but that then never happened. Laughably, and possibly fearing home reprisals, the FA demanded the replay also take place at Goodison, despite Forest earning every right to bring Newcastle back to their home turf. The Reds had no choice but to acquiesce and a single Macdonald goal sent the Magpies through. This tie had a profound effect on Forest's season as their promotion campaign fizzled out, while Newcastle went all the way to the final and a day out at Wembley where they were beaten 3-0 by Liverpool.

WE WON THE CUP

1898 FA CUP FINAL (11th April 1898) v Derby County at Crystal Palace. Won 3-1 (Arthur Capes 2, John McPherson). Forest: Dan Allsopp, Archie Ritchie, Adam Scott, Frank Forman, John McPherson (captain), Willie Wragg, Tom McInnes, Charlie Richards, Len Benbow, Arthur Capes, Alf Spouncer.

1959 FA CUP FINAL (2nd May 1959) v Luton Town at Wembley. Won 2-1 (Roy Dwight, Tommy Wilson). Forest: "Chick" Thomson, Bill Whare, Joe McDonald, Jeff Whitefoot, Bobby McKinlay, Jack Burkitt (captain), Roy Dwight, Johnny Quigley, Tommy Wilson, Billy Gray, Stewart Imlach.

1976/77 ANGLO-SCOTTISH CUP (13th December 1976 and 15th December 1976) v Leyton Orient, first leg at Brisbane Road. Drew 1-1 (John Robertson penalty). Second leg at City Ground. Won 4-0 (Colin Barrett 2, Sammy Chapman, Ian Bowyer). Forest (first leg): John Middleton, Viv Anderson, Frank Clark, John McGovern (captain), Larry Lloyd, Ian Bowyer, John O'Hare, Martin O'Neill, Peter Withe (sub Colin Barrett), Tony Woodcock, John Robertson. Forest (second leg): John Middleton, Viv Anderson, Frank Clark, John McGovern (captain), Larry Lloyd, Sammy Chapman, Martin O'Neill, Colin Barrett, Ian Bowyer, Bert Bowery, John Robertson.

1978 LEAGUE CUP FINAL AND REPLAY (18th March 1978 and 22nd March 1978) v Liverpool at Wembley. Drew 0-0. Replay at Old Trafford won 1-0 (John Robertson penalty). Forest: Chris Woods, Viv Anderson, Frank Clark, John McGovern (captain) (replaced by John O'Hare for replay), Larry Lloyd, Kenny Burns (captain in the replay), Martin O'Neill, Ian Bowyer, Peter Withe, Tony Woodcock, John Robertson.

1979 LEAGUE CUP FINAL (17th March 1979) v Southampton at Wembley. Won 3-2 (Garry Birtles 2, Tony Woodcock). Forest: Peter Shilton, Colin Barrett, Frank Clark, John McGovern (captain), Larry Lloyd, David Needham, Martin O'Neill, Archie Gemmill, Garry Birtles, Tony Woodcock, John Robertson.

1979 EUROPEAN CUP FINAL (30th May 1979) v Malmö at Olympiastadion, Munich. Won 1-0 (Trevor Francis). Forest: Peter Shilton, Viv Anderson, Frank Clark, John McGovern (captain), Larry Lloyd, Kenny Burns, Trevor Francis, Ian Bowyer, Garry Birtles, Tony Woodcock, John Robertson.

1979 SUPER CUP (30th January 1979 and 5th February 1980) v Barcelona. First leg at the City Ground. Won 1-0 (Charlie George). Second leg at the Nou Camp. Drew 1-1 (Kenny Burns). Forest (first leg): Peter Shilton, Viv Anderson, Frank Gray, Martin O'Neill, Larry Lloyd, Kenny Burns, Trevor Francis, Ian Bowyer, Garry Birtles, Charlie George, John Robertson. Forest (second leg): Peter Shilton, Viv Anderson, Frank Gray, John McGovern, Larry Lloyd, Kenny Burns, Trevor Francis (sub Martin O'Neill), Stan Bowles, Garry Birtles, Charlie George, John Robertson.

1980 EUROPEAN CUP FINAL (28th May 1980) v Hamburg at Santiago Bernabéu Stadium, Madrid. Won 1-0 (John Robertson). Forest: Peter Shilton, Viv Anderson, Frank Gray (sub Bryn Gunn), John McGovern (captain), Larry Lloyd, Kenny Burns, Martin O'Neill, Ian Bowyer, Garry Birtles, Gary Mills (sub John O'Hare), John Robertson.

1989 LEAGUE CUP FINAL (9th April 1989) v Luton Town at Wembley. Won 3-1 (Nigel Clough 2, Neil Webb). Forest: Steve Sutton, Brian Laws, Stuart Pearce (captain), Des Walker, Terry Wilson, Steve Hodge, Tommy Gaynor, Neil Webb, Nigel Clough, Lee Chapman, Garry Parker.

1989 FULL MEMBERS CUP FINAL (30th April 1989) v Everton at Wembley. Won 4-3 after extra time (Lee Chapman 2, Garry Parker 2). Forest: Steve Sutton, Brian Laws, Stuart Pearce, Des Walker, Terry Wilson, Steve Hodge (sub Steve Chettle), Tommy Gaynor (sub Franz Carr), Neil Webb, Nigel Clough, Lee Chapman, Garry Parker.

1990 LEAGUE CUP FINAL (29th April 1990) v Oldham Athletic at Wembley. Won 1-0 (Nigel Jemson). Forest: Steve Sutton, Brian Laws, Stuart Pearce, Des Walker, Steve Chettle, Steve Hodge, Gary Crosby, Garry Parker, Nigel Clough, Nigel Jemson, Franz Carr.

1992 FULL MEMBERS CUP FINAL (29th March 1992) v Southampton at Wembley. Won 3-2 after extra time (Scot Gemmill 2, Kingsley Black). Forest: Andy Marriott, Gary Charles, Stuart Pearce (sub Steve Chettle), Des Walker, Darren Wassall, Roy Keane, Gary Crosby, Scot Gemmill, Nigel Clough, Teddy Sheringham, Kingsley Black.

TRANSFER FLOPS #3

One of the saddest episodes in the career of a highly-regarded footballer came with Jim Baxter's spell at Nottingham Forest. After the surprisingly successful 1966/67 season, chairman Tony Wood announced he had ambitious plans to turn Nottingham Forest into one of Europe's top teams, saying he was going to sign a host of big names, the first of which was the ex-Rangers midfield genius Jim Baxter, who had been with a struggling Sunderland side since May 1965. Baxter signed in December 1967 as Forest's first £100,000 transfer, and manager Johnny Carey seemed obliged to play him, disrupting the Lyons–Barnwell–Baker–Wignall–Moore forward line that had served the club so well the previous season. Baxter was already battling his own demons, with his love of alcohol and the single life destroying his marriage. He played less than 50 games for the Reds, mostly unfit and unshaven, a fading shadow of the "Slim Jim" character who had come through at the end of the 1950s as Scotland's finest player for a generation. Baxter was only 29 when Forest got rid, giving him a free transfer. He returned to Rangers, expressing a desire to visit health farms to repair his pub-player physique, but it never happened. After 14 lacklustre games back at Rangers, Baxter retired. Carey was eventually sacked as the 1968/69 Forest side floundered at the bottom of the First Division, and Matt Gillies was brought in with the remit of dismantling the team of star names (such as Terry Hennessey, Henry Newton and Ian Storey-Moore) and relying on the youngsters (Liam O'Kane, Duncan McKenzie, Alan Buckley, Martin O'Neill and John Robertson) to survive. The young bloods weren't ready and Forest were relegated in 1972. Baxter himself continued to drink heavily, requiring two transplants in his 50s, and sadly died in 2001 at the age of 61.

PETER TAYLOR, FOREST GOALKEEPER

When Brian Clough's number two Peter Taylor came to the City Ground in 1976, not many people knew it was a case of a return, rather than coming to pastures new. Nottingham-born Taylor had been on Forest's books towards the end of the Second World War, and had played two games for the Reds in April 1945 in the Football League North wartime competition. Both games were against Notts County, with Forest winning 3-1 at Meadow Lane but then losing 5-2 a week later at the City Ground. Taylor remained with Forest as an amateur after the war, then signed as a professional with Coventry City in 1950. He moved to Middlesbrough in 1955, when he first encountered a brash marksman named Brian Clough. He spent a year at Port Vale then three seasons as player-manager at Burton Albion before being lured to join Clough at Hartlepools in 1965.

LIKE FATHER, LIKE GREAT-GRANDSON

The most famous name associated with Forest in their early days was Sam Weller Widdowson, inventor of the shin-guard. It's a little-known fact that Sam's great-grandson, Garry Widdowson, briefly served as an apprentice with Forest in 1976. Unfortunately for the Clifton-born youngster an injury curtailed his career before it even began.

CLOUGHIE'S FIRST CUP

At one time, a popular pub quiz question was: "What was Brian Clough's first major trophy won while manager of Nottingham Forest?" While most people would hazard a guess at the 1978 League Cup, the actual answer was the 1976/77 Anglo-Scottish Cup, although arguments would then ensue as to how such a competition qualified as "major". Forest began the 1976/77 season with a trio of qualifying ties in the tournament against Second Division rivals Notts County and top flight teams West Brom and Bristol City. Forest drew with County then beat both Albion and City to progress to the next stage, a two-legged quarter-final affair against Kilmarnock which Forest won 4-3 on aggregate. Next up were Ayr United, who included former Reds transfer flop Alex Ingram in their line-up, and a 4-1 win over two ties sent Forest to the final against Orient (as they were known at the time). In December 1976 Forest drew 1-1 with Orient at Brisbane Road, then hammered them 4-0 at home two days later to secure the silverware.

SEVENTH HEAVEN

Certainly the most unexpected result of Forest's 2011/12 campaign occurred on 20th March when the Reds went to Elland Road and hammered Leeds 7-3. Leeds actually took the lead when Ross McCormack brushed Adlene Guedioura on his way into the area and went tumbling, Robert Snodgrass converting the penalty past Lee Camp. Guedioura quickly equalised, hammering the ball home from 25 yards when there seemed little danger. The teams were about to trot in at half-time when Guedioura found Garath McCleary who bamboozled four Leeds defenders to lash in from the edge of the area. After the break Andy Reid's cross was headed in by Dexter Blackstock (51), the first of five goals in eight minutes. Leeds pulled one back through Luciano Becchio (53) then equalised via a crushing Michael Brown shot on 55. Less than a minute later a Blackstock flick gave McCleary the chance of a perfectly-struck volley that found the net from a tight angle. McCleary completed his hat-trick on 59 when found in the area by Reid, then made in 6-3 with his fourth, another tight shot. Blackstock was then given a peach of a pass by Guedioura and after a quick jink, slotted home to end a remarkable match. It was the first time Leeds had ever conceded seven at home, and the first time a team managed by Neil Warnock had ever shipped that many.

CELEBRITY FANS

Most teams are able to boast a handful of celebrity supporters, and Forest are no different, although the fans who've achieved fame while following the fortunes of the Reds are a pretty eclectic bunch. The lead singer of the Manic Street Preachers, James Dean Bradfield, is reportedly a Forest fan, as is currently one of the world's top golfers, Lee Westwood. MP Kenneth Clarke has been seen at the City Ground, but has also professed his love of Notts County, and such split loyalties do not go down so well in the football world. Su Pollard (Peggy in *Hi-de-Hi*) is a Nottingham girl and is thought to follow Forest, as is Ian Paice (drummer with Deep Purple) and, allegedly, the legendary football coach Luiz Felipe Scolari. Little-known Irish indie poppers Sultans of Ping FC were all Forest fans, releasing the flexi-disk 'Give Him a Ball and a Yard of Grass', featuring a selection of Cloughie quotes.

PLAYING FOR UNCLE SAM

In the 1970s, football, or as the American public know it, soccer, witnessed a surprising but brief surge in popularity in the States with the success of the North American Soccer League (NASL). Several Forest players enjoyed summer football in America, most famously of all perhaps Trevor Francis, whose endeavours with the Detroit Express often caused rifts between himself and Brian Clough, especially when Francis reported for pre-season training at the start of the 1979/80 season carrying an injury he had picked up in the USA. Other players who played both for Forest and NASL teams are as follows: Gary Bannister (Detroit Express), Jim Barron (Connecticut Bicentennials), Jim Baxter (Vancouver Royals), Bert Bowery (Boston Minutemen and Team Hawaii), Sammy Chapman (Tulsa Roughnecks), Peter Cormack (Toronto City), Archie Gemmill (Jacksonville Tea Men), Charlie George (Minnesota Kicks), Paddy Greenwood (Boston Minutemen), Alan Hinton (Dallas Tornado and Vancouver Whitecaps), Trevor Hockey (San Diego Jaws, San Jose Earthquakes and Las Vegas Quicksilvers), Tommy Jackson (Detroit Cougars), Len Julians (Detroit Cougars), Neil Martin (San Antonio Thunder), Jim Montgomery (Vancouver Royals), Gary Mills (Seattle Sounders), Duncan McKenzie (Tulsa Roughnecks and Chicago Sting), David Needham (Toronto Blizzard), John O'Hare (Vancouver Royals, Dallas Tornado), Steve Peplow (Chicago Sting), Jürgen Röber (Calgary Boomers), Ian Storey-Moore (Chicago Sting), Frans Thijssen (Vancouver Whitecaps), Colin Todd (Vancouver Royals, Vancouver Whitecaps), Geoff Vowden (New York Cosmos), Peter Ward (Seattle Sounders, Vancouver Whitecaps) and Peter Withe (Portland Timbers).

A CLOUGHIE JOKE

Way back in 1977, Brian Clough was once walking his dog along the banks of the River Trent when he noticed a figure struggling in the water, seemingly on the verge of drowning. Cloughie peered into the water and to his amazement, realised it was the then Notts County manager Jimmy Sirrell. Cloughie dived into the river, and as Sirrell went down for the third and final time, hauled the ancient Scot up to the surface and dragged him to the bank and out of the murky water. The pair lay there, panting on the bank, recovering their breath. Eventually, both managers regained the ability to speak. "Aye, Brian, thanks for saving my life. You, you won't tell my lads I cannae swim, will yer?" said Sirrell. "It's a deal," replied Clough, "as long as you don't tell my lads I can't walk on water."

NUMBER EIGHT IS...

Gemmill. Forest have not one but two Gemmills associated with the number eight shirt, the energetic playmaker Archie who gave his all every game for Forest's championship-winning side, and Archie's more languid son Scot, who holds the record for the most appearances for Forest wearing number eight. Archie was born in Paisley in March 1947 and joined his local side St Mirren as a youngster, and in 1966 became Scotland's first tactical substitute. A spell at Preston followed, and while at Deepdale he came to the attention of Peter Taylor, then at Derby, who informed Brian Clough, who then famously refused to leave Gemmill's house until Gemmill signed for the Rams. Gemmill spent seven years at the Baseball Ground, re-joining Clough at the City Ground in September 1977 for the surprisingly generous fee of £25,000 and Forest's second-choice goalkeeper John Middleton. Gemmill was not initially selected, with Clough insisting he wouldn't play until he had re-learnt the knack of passing the ball in any other direction than sideways. He eventually replaced Ian Bowyer, and became an integral part of the side for nearly two seasons until he wasn't selected for the 1979 European Cup final despite declaring himself fit (the same fate befell Martin O'Neill). This omission hurt Gemmill tremendously, and he was sold to Birmingham City in the summer. Clough later hinted this was a mistake, and he spent three seasons trying to replace Gemmill, with the likes of Stan Bowles and Jürgen Röber, until he succeeded with the emergence of Steve Hodge. Gemmill played out his career with Wigan and a return to Derby County. He won 43 caps for Scotland, and is best remembered, internationally, for his wonder-goal at the 1978 World Cup against Holland. He later coached at Forest and managed Rotherham. Archie's son Scotland (his actual first name) was born in Paisley in 1971 and joined Forest as an apprentice in 1987. Archie had driven his pregnant wife to Paisley from Derby to make sure Scot was born in Scotland. He became established in the Forest side in 1991 and, while never being the most appreciated Forest player of all time, went on to play over 250 games for the Reds. In 1999, with a self-imposed freeze on Forest offering new contracts, Gemmill was sold to Premiership side Everton for £250,000, where he established himself as a top flight midfielder until 2004, when he joined his dad's old team Preston, later playing for Leicester, Oxford and New Zealand Knights in Auckland. He won 26 caps for Scotland, scoring once.

THE FOREST LIBRARY

A selection of biographies and autobiographies written by Forest players and managers over the years:

Hard Man, Hard Game............................Larry Lloyd
Super Tramp.......................................John Robertson
Stan: Tackling My Demons ....Stan Collymore
My Story ....John McGovern
Cloughie: Walking on Water...................Brian Clough
The Autobiography ....Stan Bowles
Riding Through The Storm.....................Geoff Thomas
Teddy ....Teddy Sheringham
The Autobiography ....Peter Shilton
Martin O'Neill...Simon Moss
The Man with Maradona's Shirt ....Steve Hodge
Setting The Score ....Dave Bassett
The Last Fancy Dan.....................Duncan McKenzie
No Goal, No Glory....................................Peter Ward
The Party's Over...Jim Baxter
Soccer in the Blood...................................Billy Walker
Keane ....Roy Keane

FIRE!

On 24th August 1968 Forest were hosting Leeds United at the City Ground when a fire broke out in the Main Stand. Happily, there were no casualties, but most of Forest's recorded history went up in smoke, as did the club's collection of matchday programmes and other memorabilia. The score stood at 1-1 at half-time when the players noticed smoke emerging from their dressing rooms. They quickly departed and alerted the authorities, who ordered the crowd contained within the stand to move out on to the pitch. Fortunately there was no panic and the spectators moved patiently on to the field then turned to watch the Main Stand slowly and inexorably go up in smoke. As well as many of the club's historical documents, both sets of players lost all their possessions, and the Leeds United players had to march, still in muddied kit, to a local hotel. The steel framework of the stand remained standing post-fire but was clearly unsafe and had to be demolished, with a replacement stand built within two months.

A LITTLE BIT OF POLITICS

Did you know that Gordon Brown, the Prime Minister of the UK from 2007 to 2010, was also the name of a Forest player who played one game for the club in 1947 before embarking on a long and successful career with York City? And that David Cameron, who succeeded Brown in that role, was also the name of a Forest player, a centre-back who played over 20 games for the Reds in the late 1920s?

WHO'S THE EX-RED IN THE BLACK?

Steve Baines was only a brief Forest man (he made just two league appearances) but went on to have a substantial career in the lower divisions with the likes of Huddersfield, Bradford City and Chesterfield before injury forced his retirement at the age of 32. Baines then returned to the Football League, but, virtually uniquely, as a referee. Only two previous referees, Bob Matthewson and John Lloyd, had made the list after making it as professional footballers, but as that pair only amassed a total of five league appearances between them, Baines, with over 400, hugely outscored them in terms of experience. The Newark-born centre-half remained on the league list for eight years and earned a reputation for controlling games without the need to flash reds and yellows at everyone. Once off the pitch he returned to Chesterfield, helping set up the Chesterfield Football Supporters' Society.

LORENZO'S TOIL

The local press in Nottingham have never been one to ration their hyperbole, so when the headline "Forest Sign Argentine World Cup Final Hero" appeared in November 1990, Reds supporters were hardly rushing to the club shop to have "Maradona" ironed onto the back of their shirts. There was some truth in the headline though, as Brian Clough had made moves to sign defender Néstor Lorenzo, who had played all 90 minutes of the 1990 World Cup Final which Argentina lost 1-0 to West Germany. The deal fell through at the last minute though, and Lorenzo instead found himself at Swindon Town, then in the second tier, who just happened to be managed by his fellow countryman Ossie Ardiles. Less than two years later Lorenzo was back in his homeland after signing for San Lorenzo.

THE FULHAM MARATHON

One of Brian's Clough's first jobs as Forest boss was to guide his new charges through the early rounds of the FA Cup. His first game was against Tottenham Hotspur at White Hart Lane, a replay of the third round tie that had been drawn four days previously (before Clough had taken over). Forest won that one 1-0, and were drawn against fellow Second Division side Fulham in round four. The first match ended 0-0 at Craven Cottage, mainly thanks to the resilience of Forest's centre-back pairing Sammy Chapman and John Cottam and the bluntness of the Reds' striking duo Barry Butlin and Neil Martin. The return at the City Ground on 3rd February also ended all-square, with Jimmy Dowie scoring for the Cottagers just before half-time, then Neil Martin equalising on 65. Extra time failed to determine a result, so it was back to Craven Cottage two days later. Fulham again took the lead, this time through Alan Slough, but John Robertson's curling free-kick two minutes into the second half brought Forest level. It was 1-1 after 90 minutes and still the same score after the extra period. Time for game four, on 10th February, and yet again Fulham took the lead, this time through striker Viv Busby on the half-hour. Busby scored again on 55 and although Chapman pulled one back 11 minutes later Forest finally ran out of fuel. Fulham therefore emerged victorious after over seven hours of football, and went on to the final where they lost to West Ham. A league game at Craven Cottage on 11th January meant that of Brian Clough's first nine games in charge of Forest, five of them had been against Fulham.

FORE!

Seventies Forest striker Duncan McKenzie was a man of many talents, most of them naturally displayed on the football field, but was also a fine cricketer, snooker player and darts player as well as being an adept horse-rider. At one time the legend followed him around that he had jumped over a (parked) Mini as a 15-year-old, and he once repeated the trick in front of 30,000 at Elland Road while a Leeds United player. He also possessed the crucial knack of throwing a golf ball the entire length of a football pitch, as he proved at the 115-yards-long City Ground in 1973.

AS LUCK WOULD HAVE IT

In March 1970, Forest coaches Alan Hill and Bob McKinlay were summoned to Eastwood armed with the insider knowledge that Priory Celtic's under-14 goalkeeper was a bit special. They liked what they saw, but what they saw there and liked was Celtic's young blonde curly-haired 13-year-old midfielder. They met with the youngster after the game and despite finding him a quiet lad, invited him along for a trial at Forest, and he later signed apprentice forms in 1972. The player in question was Tony Woodcock, who would go one to be one of the key pieces in Forest's 1977/78 championship-winning side.

DAS BOAT

For some obscure reason, Consolidated Fisheries in Grimsby decided in 1973 to name a fleet of their trawlers after famous football clubs. Naturally, Forest were among the clubs chosen to be so honoured, along with footballing giants such as Carlisle United, Gillingham and Real Madrid. A delighted Forest committee asked for a picture of said boat, which was duly received. Delight turned to indignation when said photo revealed the boat had not been called Nottingham Forest, Forest or even Nottm Forest, but Notts Forest. Incidentally, a trawler named Notts County was sunk off the coast of Iceland in 1969, eerily predicting the gloomy future largely well beneath the waves of the top flight of Nottingham's second side.

IT'S A MARATHON, NOT A SPRINT...

...so says one of football's most oft-repeated quotes, but this was perhaps best emphasised in the elongated 1946/47 season, which, for Forest at least, began on 31st August 1946 and ended on 14th June 1947. Most of the blame for this prolonged term could be placed on the atrocious weather of the winter of 1947, which for weeks made playing football impossible. Between 1st February and 15th March Forest managed one solitary league game, a 1-1 draw at Leicester City, while the country battled horrendous and endless snowstorms followed by flooding once the snow began to thaw. Forest played 13 league games in April, May and June, culminating in a 4-0 win at home to Bradford Park Avenue in which Tom Johnston scored a hat-trick.

WE'LL MEET AGAIN

One of the club's most loyal servants, Jack Burkitt, was rewarded for his distinguished service for the Reds in 1961 with a testimonial. The team chosen for the game were Forest's first-ever Swedish opponents, Malmö. Of course, just under 20 years later these two sides would meet again in the 1979 European Cup Final. Forest won both games, the former 5-1 (although the match was curtailed due to fog) and the latter 1-0.

SOUR TIMES

Christmas 1973 was not a pleasant time to be in England. The power crisis fuelled by the rise in oil prices and striking miners held the country in its grip, with constant power cuts and three-day weeks becoming factors of everyday life. Forest were hit as hard as any other club, and in the final matchday programme before Christmas Day solemnly announced that due to the crisis, they'd been forced to turn the power to the clock on the scoreboard off.

I'M JUST A LOVE MACHINE

One of the most interestingly-named players ever to play for Forest was tough inside-forward Johnny Love, who signed for the club in February 1949 from Albion Rovers for £8,000. Love was also one of the few players to play for the Reds with military honours, winning a Distinguished Flying Cross while serving with the RAF in 1944. Love was a regular in the side until 1951 when he lost his first team place to "Tucker" Johnson, and he joined Llanelli as player-manager in 1952. He also managed Walsall and Wrexham.

A LITTLE BIT OF BULLY

In the early-1970s sports such as darts and snooker spiralled in popularity, mainly thanks to television coverage and, in snooker's case definitely, the advent of colour TV. In 1972 Forest held their first darts competition, which was won by the club's uber-sportsman Duncan McKenzie, who beat Peter Hindley in the final. The following season McKenzie wasn't so successful, losing in the final to Barry Lyons. The 1974 competition was won by John Middleton, and sadly no further competitions were reported upon.

PFA PLAYER OF THE YEAR

The Professional Footballers' Association began handing out awards at their AGM in 1974, giving prizes to their Footballer of the Year, Young Footballer of the Year and an All-Star team for each division. The only Forest player to win the main award was Peter Shilton in 1977/78, although how Stuart Pearce didn't win it in 1991 after an excellent season when bouncing back from his Italia 90 issue is anyone's guess. Tony Woodcock is Forest's sole winner of the Young Player award. Duncan McKenzie was the first Forest man to make an appearance in an All-Star team. Peter Shilton (who was the First Division's selected goalkeeper in the All-Star team every season he was at Forest) and Stuart Pearce share the honour of the most Forest appearances in the All-Star team at five apiece. A full list of All-Star appearances is given below:

Duncan McKenzie .... (Second Division 1973/74)
John Robertson ..... (Second Division 1976/77; First Division 1977/78)
Peter Shilton (First Division 1977/78, 1978/79, 1979/80, 1980/81, 1981/82)
Viv Anderson .... (First Division 1978/79, 1979/80)
Garry Birtles ....(First Division 1980/81)
Stuart Pearce (First Division 1987/88, 1988/89, 1989/90, 1990/91, 1991/92)
Des Walker ....(First Division 1987/88, 1989/90, 1990/91, 1991/92)
Steve Hodge ....(First Division 1989/90)
Roy Keane ....(Premiership 1992/93)
Colin Cooper .... (First Division 1993/94, 1997/98)
Scot Gemmill ....(First Division 1993/94)
Stan Collymore ....(First Division 1993/94)
Steve Stone ....(Premiership 1995/96)
Pierre van Hooijdonk ....(First Division 1997/98)
Michael Dawson ....(First Division 2002/03)
David Johnson ....(First Division 2002/03)
Andy Reid ....(First Division 2003/04)
Ian Breckin .... (League 1 2006/07)
Julian Bennett .... (League 1 2007/08)
Kris Commons .... (League 1 2007/08)
Lee Camp ....(Championship 2009/10)
Chris Gunter ....(Championship 2009/10)
Wes Morgan ....(Championship 2010/11)

THE COUNTY CUP

The Nottinghamshire County Cup was an annual cup competition run on a haphazard basis between Nottinghamshire's three professional sides (and, in the first three seasons, the winners of the Notts Senior Cup, who each time were Newark Town). At the competition's peak attendances matched those of league games (the 1966/67 final attracted a crowd of 22,851), but as Forest began to compete in Europe attendances dwindled, as did the frequency of the competition due to fixture congestion. There came a brief revival of consistency in the 1980s but ridiculous delays to matches (the 1994/95 final was eventually played in the 1996/97 season) continued and in 2002 the competition hit the dust. Forest's complete record is given below:

1936/37 .... Final, lost to Notts County (A) 1-0
1937/38 .... Final, lost to Mansfield Town (A) 2-1
1938/39 .... Shared, drew with Mansfield Town (H) 2-2
1960/61 .... WINNERS, beat Notts County (H) 4-3
1961/62 .... WINNERS, beat Mansfield Town (H) 3-2
1962/63 .... Final, lost to Notts County (H) 2-1
1963/64 .... WINNERS, beat Notts County (A) 5-1
1964/65 .... WINNERS, beat Mansfield Town (H) 5-0
1966/67 .... WINNERS, beat Notts County (H) 2-0
1967/68 .... WINNERS, beat Notts County (H) 3-0
1968/69 .... WINNERS, beat Notts County (H) 2-1
1969/70 .... WINNERS, beat Notts County (H) 2-0
1970/71 ....Final, lost to Mansfield Town (H) 1-0
1971/72 ....Semi-final, lost to Notts County (A) 3-0
1972/73 .... WINNERS, beat Mansfield Town (A) 1-0
1973/74 .... WINNERS, beat Notts County (H) 3-2
1974/75 ....Final, lost to Notts County (H) 1-0
1975/76 .... Final, lost to Notts County (A) 1-0
1976/77 .... WINNERS, beat Notts County on penalties
1977/78 .... WINNERS, beat Mansfield Town (H) 4-0
1978/79 .... WINNERS, beat Mansfield Town (H) 3-1
1979/80 .... WINNERS, beat Notts County (A) 2-1
1980/81 .... WINNERS, beat Mansfield Town (H) 2-1
1981/82 .... WINNERS, beat Notts County (H) 7-1

1982/83 ....WINNERS, beat Notts County (H) 4-3
1983/84 ....WINNERS, beat Notts County (H) 3-0
1984/85 ....Final, lost to Notts County (H) 2-1
1985/86 ....WINNERS, beat Notts County (H) 2-0
1986/87 .... Final, lost to Mansfield Town on penalties
1987/88 ....Semi-final, lost to Notts County on penalties
1988/89 ....Semi-final, lost to Notts County on penalties
1989/90 ....WINNERS, beat Mansfield Town (A) 4-0
1990/91 ....WINNERS, beat Mansfield Town (H) 5-0
1992/93 ....WINNERS, beat Notts County (H) 3-0
1993/94 ....WINNERS, beat Notts County (H) 3-1
1994/95 .... Final, lost to Notts County (H) on penalties
1997/98 .... WINNERS, beat Notts County (A) 6-1
1998/99 ....WINNERS, beat Notts County (H) 5-0
1999/00 ....WINNERS, beat Notts County (H) 1-0
2000/01 ....WINNERS, beat Notts County (H) 1-0
2001/02 ....WINNERS, beat Notts County (H) 1-0

BLACK IS (NOT) THE COLOUR

For the 1973/74 season, Forest decided to ditch their traditional red socks for black, a move unpopular with supporters as Forest's kit, to all intents and purposes, became perfectly identical to Manchester United's. Several of the players were not in favour either, and left-back John Winfield's ire was such that the rest of the squad nicknamed him "Johnny Redsocks". The black socks were ditched after one season and red stockings have remained the norm ever since.

BET YOU'RE SORRY NOW

The prolonged 1973/74 FA Cup quarter-final tie between Forest and Newcastle, which was marred by the invasion of Newcastle fans in the first game when Forest were 3-1 up and was eventually won in the second neutral replay by the Magpies, naturally caused a deal of ill feeling between the teams. However, Forest could hardly claim the moral high ground when a request came from Newcastle to cancel a meaningless reserve team game against Forest on the same day as the first team's semi-final against Burnley so that the players and officials could attend the game. Forest refused and the second-strings played out a 1-1 draw as United beat Burnley 2-0 at Hillsborough.

LET'S BE FRANK

Despite only playing for the club for two seasons, Scottish left-back Frank Gray contributes a trio of interesting snippets when it comes to Forest. Firstly, with his appearance in the 1980 European Cup Final for Forest against Hamburg, Gray became the first player to appear in European Cup finals for two different English teams, having played for Leeds United in the 1975 final loss to Bayern Munich. Gray is also the only Forest player to compete on the televised BBC sports competition *Superstars* (although Dave Beasant later appeared in the revised version on Five as the goalkeeper in the football skills event). Finally, Gray's son, Andy, was signed by Forest in 1998 and spent four years at the club, becoming one of the few father-son combinations to play for Forest in their history.

INTERNATIONAL BOSSES

Whereas many Forest players have gone on to manage at league level, hardly any have actually gone on to manage an international side. The first to do so was probably Tom Bradshaw, a winger who played for Forest for a year in 1897, then managed Holland, albeit for a single game in 1913, a 4-2 defeat in Zwolle against Belgium. Forest's 1960s striker Frank Wignall had a spell in charge of the Qatari national side, whereas much more recently the Forest legend Stuart Pearce took temporary charge of the England team in 2012 following the resignation of Fabio Capello, until the appointment of Roy Hodgson in May.

CLOUGHIE AT THE CUP FINAL

Thanks to Brian and Nigel, the name Clough will forever be synonymous with Nottingham Forest. However, Brian Clough's appointment early in 1975 was not the first time the name Clough had become associated with the club's successes. In 1959, when Forest beat Luton 2-1 in the FA Cup Final at Wembley, the referee was Jack Clough. The Bolton-born Fifa official was no relation to the – at the time – Middlesbrough striker who later took charge at Forest with unparalleled success. Curiously, Clough was one of the names mentioned by the then Reds boss Billy Walker as a potential signing funded by the cup win, but instead he plumped for Wolverhampton Wanderers striker Colin Booth.

NUMBER NINE IS...

Joe Baker. Many a fine specimen of a player has graced the number nine shirt for Nottingham Forest, but perhaps none more popular than Joe "The King" Baker. A Liverpudlian by birth, Baker spent his childhood in Motherwell, began his career with Hibernian and became the first player to play for England without ever playing for an English team. After scoring over 100 goals for Hibs, Baker joined Torino in 1961 but had an unhappy time there, and joined his first English club, Arsenal, in 1962. His prolific ability returned and he was the top scorer at Highbury for three of his four seasons there. Johnny Carey snapped him up for Forest in 1966 for a fee of £65,000. Baker swiftly settled into the role of centre-forward and crowd favourite, impressing with his goalscoring prowess and ability on the ball, and becoming an integral part of the team that finished runners-up in 1966/67 and reached the FA Cup semi-finals. The Forest support broke into the cry of "zigger zagga" whenever Baker received the ball, anticipating one of his mazy runs through the defence. That great late-1960s team began to dismantle under the control of Matt Gillies, and in 1969 Baker was sold to Sunderland. He stayed at Roker Park for two seasons before returning to his spiritual homeland at Hibernian but moved to Raith Rovers in 1972. He retired in 1974 with an excellent record of 301 goals in 507 games, moving outside the game to become a publican, although he had two spells as manager at Albion Rovers in the 1980s. In 2003 the shocking news arrived that Baker had died at the early age of 63 after suffering a heart attack during a charity golf tournament.

THE FIRST AND THE LAST

The first and final Forest sides Brian Clough selected: 8th January 1975 v Tottenham Hotspur (FA Cup third round replay). 1-0 (Martin). John Middleton, Liam O'Kane, Paddy Greenwood (sub John Cottam), Sammy Chapman, David Jones, Paul Richardson, George Lyall, Neil Martin, Barry Butlin, Ian Bowyer, Martin O'Neill. 8th May 1993 v Ipswich Town (Premiership) 1-2 (Clough penalty). Andy Marriott, Brian Laws, Brett Williams, Steve Chettle, Carl Tiler, Roy Keane, Kingsley Black (Toddy Örlygsson), Scot Gemmill, Nigel Clough, Lee Glover, Ian Woan.

THE LEAGUE OF NATIONS

Aside from the four home nations and Ireland, at the time of writing 56 players from 26 different countries have played from Forest as overseas players. The full list is: Adlène Guedioura (Algeria), Gino Padula (Argentina), Alan Davidson and Gareth Edds (Australia), Davy Oyen (Belgium), George Elokobi (Cameroon), Jim Brennan (Canada), Nikola Jerkan (Croatia), Rune Pedersen and Mikkel Beck (Denmark), Carlos Merino (Spain), David Friio, Vincent Fernandez, Thierry Bonalair, Jean-Claude Darcheville, Bernard Allou, Guy Moussi and Matthieu Louis-Jean (France), Jürgen Röber, Eugen Bopp and Felix Bastians (Germany), Junior Agogo (Ghana), Andrea Silenzi, Salvatore Matrecano, Moreno Mannini and Gianluca Petrachi (Italy), Eugene Dadi (Ivory Coast), Darryl Powell, Marlon King and David Johnson (Jamaica), Pierre van Hooijdonk, Bryan Roy, Hans van Breukelen, Frans Thijssen, George Boateng, Hans Segers and Johnny Metgod (Netherlands), Dele Adebola (Nigeria), Einar Aas, Lars Bohinen, Alf-Inge Håland, Ståle Stensaas, Kjetil Osvold and Jon Olav Hjelde (Norway), Radi Majewski (Poland), Hugo Porfirio (Portugal), Arthur Lightening (South Africa), Marco Pascolo and Raimondo Ponte (Switzerland), Jesper Mattson (Sweden), Yoann Folly (Togo), Stern John (Trinidad and Tobago), and Robbie Findley, Jon-Paul Pittman, Ben Olsen and John Harkes (USA). Dexter Blackstock was selected for the Antigua and Barbuda international side in 2012, but was born in Oxford.

53 X 5 = CONSISTENCY

In the rather uneventful 1970/71 season, Forest played 42 league games, five FA Cup ties, three League Cup ties, two Texaco Cup matches and one County Cup game, and, remarkably, five players – almost the entire defence – played in every one of them. Goalkeeper Jim Barron, full-backs Peter Hindley and John Winfield, right-half Sammy (then still known as Bob) Chapman and centre-half Liam O'Kane all completed 100% records in all competitions. The only remaining defensive position, left-half, was shared between Henry Newton (who was transferred to Everton in October 1970), Tommy Jackson (who came from Everton as part of the Newton deal) and Doug Fraser.

TAKEN FOR GRANTED

Brian Grant was a left-back who, despite some early promise, failed to quite make the grade with Forest in the early-1960s. He was sold in 1965 to Hartlepools United, and would later see service at Bradford City and Cambridge United. A pretty unremarkable career then, that became more interesting a decade or so later – Grant was the first signing for Hartlepools United's fledging managerial team, who, as you've probably guessed by now, were Brian Clough and Peter Taylor.

BOB'S NOT YOUR AUNTIE

Brian Clough's public condemnation of Justin Fashanu's poor effort during one of his early games, a 4-3 defeat by Birmingham City at St Andrew's, did not go down well with a few people, least of all the writer of a letter to the Forest matchday programme for a following game against Sunderland. The lady writer could not claim, however, complete impartiality in her complaint, as the note came from Justin's auntie, Norga Untalim.

FOREST – LIVE!

Nottingham Forest are a team with a habit of collecting firsts, so it seems highly appropriate that they were involved in the first live televised Football League match on TV, which took place on 2nd October 1983. Forest were visiting Tottenham Hotspur, and despite taking the lead through Colin Walsh after five minutes, ended up beaten as Spurs fought back to win 2-1 with goals by Gary Stevens (70) and Steve Archibald (85). Forest: Hans van Breukelen, Viv Anderson, Kenny Swain, Colin Todd, Paul Hart, Ian Bowyer, Steve Wigley, Peter Davenport, Garry Birtles, Steve Hodge, Colin Walsh.

DAZED DANZEY

Brian Clough was never the type to shy away from the unorthodox. As Forest marched out on to the pitch for the 1989 Littlewoods Cup Final against Luton Town, 99.9% of Reds fans failed to recognise one face among the likes of Des Walker, Neil Webb and Nigel Clough. Was it a last-minute signing or an emergency change at the 11th hour? No, it was youth team striker Mick Danzey, who, as a reward for being Brian Clough's dogsbody for the final, was trotted out among the playing personnel at Wembley for the pre-game line-up.

SHOOT SPAV!

Every generation of Forest support throughout history has had its heroes – from Sam Widdowson and Grenville Morris to Joe Baker and Stuart Pearce – and the main man for the Reds in the 1920s was John Richard Spaven, known as Jack. "Spav", as he was affectionately called, was an inside-right known for his rocket-powered boots, and the home crowd used to yell "shoot Spav" whenever he had the ball close to goal. Spaven was born in Scarborough and began his career with Goole Town but spent the war with the Royal Horse Artillery in France. He played for Scunthorpe after the war then joined Forest in 1921, helping the club to promotion in 1922. He moved to Grantham at the end of 1925/26 after 170 games and 50 goals, then took over the running of the Lord Nelson pub in Nottingham in 1931. Spaven remained a Forest fan, frequently visiting the City Ground until his death in 1970 aged 79.

NOT GOOD ENOUGH?

Of those who played in the successful 1959 FA Cup Final for the Reds against Luton Town, the one who perhaps cherished the occasion most was inside-right Johnny Quigley. Quigley's career looked to have been over before it had actually begun, released by Celtic at the age of 20 in 1956 after being told he wasn't good enough for senior football. He then suffered the indignity of being sold by Celtic's junior side, St Anthony's, to rivals Ashfield for a few pounds. However, things took a positive turn just a few days later when he was spotted by Forest manager Billy Walker and invited for a trial. Less than a month later Quigley made the Forest first team and played for them regularly in the top flight until 1965.

SENT TO COVENTRY

Over the years there seems to have been an unfeasible amount of transfer activity between Forest and Coventry City. Sent from Forest to Coventry have been Colin Collindridge, Tommy Capel, Ron Farmer, Ken Simcoe, Noel Simpson, Alan Moore, Arthur Lemon, Arthur Lightening, Peter Hindley, Jim McInally and Andy Impey. Making the reverse journey have been Neil Martin, Larry Lloyd, Ian Wallace, Ian Butterworth, Stuart Pearce, Robert Rosario and Marcus Hall, meaning a total of 18 transfers between the sides.

NUMBER TEN IS...

Stan Collymore. The chant "there's only one Stan Collymore" is not strictly true in this case, as Collymore's father was also called Stanley, a Barbadian who met his mother in Cannock. The couple moved to Barbados but returned to Staffordshire where Stan junior was born in Stone, in 1971. A Villa fan, striker Collymore tried his luck at Walsall and Wolves before drifting into non-league football with Stafford Rangers. Crystal Palace handed him a professional contract in 1990 but with Ian Wright and Mark Bright forming a legendary partnership, Collymore dropped to the third tier in 1992 to sign for Southend United. It was at Roots Hall that Collymore found his shooting boots, so much so that Brian Clough considered signing him for Forest as they blundered towards relegation in 1993 but baulked at the £2m asking price. In the summer of 1993 Frank Clark was not so afraid to flash his wallet and Stan was a Forest man. Collymore possessed pace and strength, the ability to beat defenders and a lethal shot from either foot. The sight of Collymore with the ball approaching quivering defenders was one that Forest fans soon became accustomed to. In his brief term, Collymore scored 41 goals in 65 games and became football's most wanted property. Despite finishing third in the top flight and qualifying for Europe in 1994/95, Collymore needed a bigger stage than Forest to display his talents and he joined Liverpool for £8.5m. After a promising start he found himself at odds with the laddish culture at Anfield at the time, alienating him from his team-mates, and his career began to drift as he battled many personal demons. After leaving Liverpool in 1997 he would only play 73 more games (and score 14 goals) before announcing his retirement in 2001 while at Real Oviedo aged 30. It was an unfortunate and premature end to a career that promised so much, but Collymore has publicly stated he was satisfied with what he achieved and has since forged a successful career in the media.

DON'T GO BREAKING YOUR LEG

In terms of famous relations, very few Forest players are likely to be able to beat Roy Dwight, hero of Forest's 1959 FA Cup win who scored the first goal then was carried off with a broken leg. His cousin? Pop legend Elton John.

HAPPY NEW YEAR

The Forest matchday programme for the New Year's Day game at home to Newcastle celebrated the turn of the year with a front cover photograph of the club's Scottish playing contingent, namely Brian Rice (born in Bellshill, Glasgow), Terry Wilson (born in Broxburn, near Edinburgh) and Lee Glover (born in Kettering, Northamptonshire, but of Scottish descent), all splendidly bedecked in green and black tartan kits. Unfortunately, the Scottishness of the trio was called into question a few weeks later, when a reader wrote to the programme and pointed out that all three of the players were in fact wearing the traditional Scottish dress back to front.

MISTAKEN IDENTITY?

Brian Clough was always fond of the odd jape with the media while in charge at the City Ground. In December 1988, after Forest had beaten Leicester City 2-1 at home in a League Cup fourth round replay, the Central TV crew who were covering the game were keen to interview the man of the match Franz Carr, Forest's speedster wing-man. Instead of Carr, Clough sent out 17-year-old reserve Shaun Browne who, even with a quick splash of water to mimic perspiration, bore only a passing resemblance to the Reds' number seven. The Central TV crew failed to twig the send-up and Browne gave an excellent bluffing performance.

ROOTING FOR TOOTING

Forest's FA Cup run of 1959 was one that was almost over before it had begun. The Reds' third round opponents were amateur side Tooting and Mitcham, then playing in the Isthmian League, and who had already pitched Bournemouth and Northampton out of the competition. The game took place at Tooting's Sandy Lane ground on 10th January 1959 in atrocious weather and on a heavily rutted and frozen pitch. A crowd approaching 14,000 cheered the non-leaguers to a 2-0 lead through Albert Grainger and Ted Murphy at half-time. Forest boss Billy Walker instructed his players to abandon their game-plan and "play like Tooting". It worked, as Forest pulled it back to level with a Murphy own goal and a Billy Gray penalty. This brought Tooting to the City Ground, where a massive crowd of 42,362 witnessed Forest comfortably beat the amateurs 3-0.

SELDOM SEEN SCOTS

For a period in the late-1980s, Forest picked up an odd habit of signing players from Scotland, then never giving them a chance in the first team before being sold for a loss a season or two later. The first of these was Martin Clark, who cost £80,000 from Clyde, where his father John was manager, in 1989. Clark never received a sniff of the first team, and was sold to Mansfield Town in 1990. Next up was the Dunfermline winger Mark Smith, signed in 1990, then sold to Shrewsbury Town in 1991. Most (in)famously of all was the next signing, Morton's attacking midfielder Alan Mahood who, despite only playing nine games for the Greenock side, was already being described as the "new Kenny Dalglish". Mahood failed to buck the trend though, and was sent back to Morton a year later. In 1992 Brian Clough really pushed the boat out with a £750,000 splash on Dundee United's midfielder Ray McKinnon. McKinnon finally bucked the trend by actually playing for the first team, making six appearances (and scoring once) during the disastrous 1992/93 season. McKinnon remained at Forest until 1994, when he was sold to Aberdeen.

THREE AND OUT

Forest strikers Grenville Morris, Thomas Roe and Ian Wallace all scored at least one hat-trick for Forest during their respective periods at the club, but all these feats share the same trait. Morris scored three against Sheffield Wednesday on 11th December 1909, Roe against Manchester City on 24th September 1927 and Wallace against Birmingham City on 5th September 1981. What made these feats unique is that they were all futile as Forest were the losing team on each occasion. Wednesday and Birmingham beat Forest 4-3, while Manchester City hammered the Reds 5-4.

NOTTINGHAM WHITE SOX

As a one-off, and as suggested as an experiment by ex-Forest goalkeeper and the then coach Alan Hill, the Reds donned white socks – a complete change from the traditional red – for a Milk Cup tie at Wimbledon, then in the third tier. Hill's explanation for the change was simply that he thought the players would prefer playing in white stockings. He was wrong – Forest lost 2-0 and the experiment was never repeated.

HOW THE MIGHTY HAVE FALLEN

The Nottingham Forest of 1982 were quite different from the team that had been a major force between 1977 and 1980, but they were still supposed to make light work of visiting Wrexham in the first round of the FA Cup on New Year's Day. Forest sat seventh in the First Division, while Wrexham were being propped up only by Orient and Grimsby from the bottom of the tier below. It began so well for the Reds as well, with a Mark Proctor goal after only two minutes, but Wrexham equalised via Steve Dowman just past the hour. Ex-Notts County man Mick Vinter gave Wrexham the lead on 70, then three minutes later the vastly experienced marksman Dixie McNeill gave them a two-goal cushion, one they maintained to the final whistle. Those guilty Forest men: Peter Shilton, Viv Anderson, Bryn Gunn, David Needham, Willie Young, Colin Walsh, Jürgen Röber (sub John McGovern), Ian Wallace, Peter Ward, Mark Proctor, John Robertson. So appalled was Brian Clough about his team's display he immediately arranged a friendly against the strongest opposition available for the Monday after the match. The same 11 took the field against Luton and partially redeemed their reputation with a 5-1 thrashing of the Hatters.

SEMI-FINAL WOE

Following their 1959 FA Cup Final victory, the next time Forest came anywhere close to Wembley was seven years later, when the great 1966/67 side landed a semi-final at Hillsborough against Tottenham Hotspur on 29th April 1967. Despite Forest being on course for the runners-up spot in the top flight, Spurs entered the game as slight favourites, mainly due to the unavailability of Forest's Joe Baker, who had been injured in the previous round against Everton. Indeed, it was Spurs, fielding two future Forest bosses in their line-up in Joe Kinnear and Dave Mackay, who triumphed in front of 55,000 spectators. The eternal Forest nemesis, Jimmy Greaves, put Spurs up on the half-hour, then Frank Saul smashed home a shot on 67. Terry Hennessey headed home a Barry Lyons corner for Forest on 75 but it was not to be for the Reds. Spurs packed their defence and held out to earn a trip to Wembley, where they beat Chelsea 2-1 in the final. Forest would not reach a further FA Cup semi-final for 20 years.

THE NOTTINGHAM CUP

In the early years of football, Nottingham could boast a whole host of "major" sides. As professionalism took over in the late 1880s, players were more likely to play for clubs with the necessary funds to pay them, hence most of these teams folded, leaving only Forest and neighbours County. In 1883 a tournament took place, known variously as the Nottingham Cup or Notts Cup, to ascertain who held bragging rights in the city. Forest brushed past Notts Swifts, Notts Rangers and Notts Olympic to take on Notts Trent in the final. They could only draw 1-1 at the Castle Ground, but won the replay 5-1. Just for good measure, Forest had played Notts (as they were known then before they added the official County suffix) in the FA Cup, but had lost 3-0. The following season Forest were the winners again, beating Basford Rovers in the final 6-1, with Tinsley Lindley netting a hat-trick, after beating United Amateurs and Notts Olympic en route. Forest made it a hat-trick in 1885/86, defeating Nottingham Rangers in the final, and won it again the following season, beating Nottingham Olympic 3-0 at home to retain their trophy. This was the last time the competition was played, meaning Forest could boast a 100% record in the four seasons the tournament was run.

TERRIFIC TINSLEY

While not official as many of Forest's early games were reported without the listing of goalscorers, it is thought the record for the number of goals scored by a Forest player in a single game is seven, achieved by Tinsley Lindley in a friendly against Sheffield on 13th October 1883. The record for an official game is five, achieved by "Sandy" Higgins in the record 14-0 defeat by Forest of Clapton in the first round of the FA Cup on 17th January 1891.

IT'S CERTAINLY NOT CRICKET

On 5th May 1955 Forest took on Nottingham Rugby Football Club in a bizarre friendly at the City Ground for charity. Undecided perhaps on which code should be followed, the team played football, but with a rugby ball. A crowd of 1,100 witnessed a 3-0 Reds victory, with goals from John Langford, Jack Burkitt and Geoff Thomas.

WHISTLE HAPPY

The referee for Forest's 2-1 loss at Sunderland on 26th September 1908 was Mr JH Smith of Doncaster. Nothing unusual there, but said official made a silly mistake during the game and came up with an unusual method of rectifying it. As the teams took the field for the second half, Mr Smith owned up to blowing for half-time two minutes early. The referee ordered both teams to play from the same end as they had played in the first, blew up again two minutes later, and got the bemused players to now change ends.

MOST INTERNATIONALS?

A decent trivia question to flummox a Forest fan would be: "When was the City Ground home to the most number of international players?" No doubt, most Reds fans would plump for the heady days of the late seventies, but the correct answer would be on 14th June 1996 when a total of 28 internationals were seen on the City Ground pitch during the European Championship match between Portugal and Turkey. This was the middle game of three the City Ground hosted during the tournament, the others involving the aforementioned teams and Croatia. The City Ground had hosted an international game before, albeit an unofficial wartime one between England and Wales in 1941, which England won 4-1 helped by four goals from Charlton's Don Welsh. Incidentally, one of the players who appeared at the City Ground during Euro 96, Nikola Jerkan, became a Red as Frank Clark snapped the defender up for £1m when the tournament concluded. Jerkan seldom impressed and was released to the Belgian side Charleroi in 1999.

CAREER CURTAILED

In 1972, the shocking news came to the footballing world that the England goalkeeper Gordon Banks had lost the sight in his right eye following a car crash. This, to Forest, came as a tragic coincidence, as two of their youngsters, Steve Baines and Tommy White, had too been involved in a car crash a week earlier. While Baines only suffered minor injuries, White's face was severely lacerated, requiring 50 stitches, and he too lost the sight in one eye. The highly-promising forward had no choice but to call time on his career after just one substitute appearance.

THE NUMBER 58

Did you know that for many years, Forest in cup draws were always represented by the number 58? In the early-1960s the FA drew up an alphabetical list of clubs and numbered each side accordingly, with Forest of course being 58th on the list. This system was maintained even when the member clubs of the league changed, as it did when Bradford Park Avenue (number 12) and Barrow (number five) lost their membership in 1970 and 1972 respectively. Instead of the whole list being redrawn and numbers reallocated, the clubs' replacements, Cambridge United and Hereford United, were allocated the numbers 92 and 94.

FOREST'S FIRST PLAYER-MANAGER...

...but not quite. When Dave Mackay agreed to take his Forest side to play Derby in a testimonial for the Rams' long-serving former Wales international midfield player Alan Durban in September 1973, he initially promised to take the field as a Forest player during the game. Sadly, Mackay didn't fulfil his promise, as the match was postponed for five months dues to Derby's exploits in the European Cup. When it was eventually played, the game ended 1-1 with Forest's goal coming from a George Lyall penalty, and Mackay must have enjoyed revisiting his own ground as less than a month later he was back as Derby County's manager.

WE'LL MEET AGAIN

On 7th August 1970 Forest played Hamburger SV in a friendly at the City Ground, which the Reds won 1-0 thanks to a Peter Cormack goal. Anyone suggesting at the time that the same two teams would be meeting just less than a decade later in the European Cup Final would, of course, have been dismissed as delusional, although of course that is exactly what happened on that famous day in Madrid.

YOU'LL BE BACK

On 28th November 1970, Brian Clough brought his youthful and talented Derby County side to the City Ground and hammered Forest 4-2. Derby's scorers that day were Archie Gemmill (two), John O'Hare and John McGovern, all three of who, would form part of Clough's Nottingham Forest championship-winning side in 1978.

LIKE FATHER, LIKE DAUGHTER

Many sons, of course, follow in their footballer fathers' imprints and become professionals themselves. However, not so many daughters do. One father-daughter combination who both made it to the highest sphere of their sports were former Forest left-back or centre-back Bryn Gunn and his daughter Jenny. Bryn made his debut for Forest as a 17-year-old in 1975 but never really held down a regular place until seven years later. He spent over a decade with the club, making 131 appearances, the pinnacle of his career no doubt his substitute appearance in the 1980 European Cup Final against Hamburg. Jenny was born in Nottingham in 1986 and after excelling at cricket as a youngster, played for England aged 17. She played eight Tests for her country but close to one hundred one-day internationals.

CHARITY BEGINS AT HOME

Forest have played in the FA Charity (now Community) Shield twice. In 1959 Forest, as the cup holders, played Wolves, league champions, at Molineux, and lost 3-1 with Tommy Wilson scoring for the Reds. Nineteen years later Forest (as league champions) fared much better as they hammered the FA Cup holders Ipswich Town 5-0 at Wembley, goals coming from Martin O'Neill (two), Peter Withe, Larry Lloyd and John Robertson.

CUP HOLDERS CUT DOWN BY THE BLADES

30th January 1960 was the last time in Forest's history that they could claim the title of FA Cup holders. After winning the trophy in 1959, Forest went out the following season on this day to Sheffield United, soundly beaten 3-0 by the then Second Division side. More than 60 years later, it's a title that Forest have exceedingly infrequently come close to re-obtaining. Curiously, when Forest won the Cup in 1898, the team that knocked their hands off the trophy the following season was – Sheffield United. The Reds lost 1-0 at home to the Blades in the quarter-final. United would go on all the way to the final where they defeated Derby County, who had been defeated by Forest in the final the previous season, United winning 4-1 at Crystal Palace. The United of 1960 were not so fortunate though, losing to their neighbours Wednesday in the quarter-final.

NUMBER ELEVEN IS...

John Robertson. Forest fans can be split into two categories; those who think John Robertson is the greatest-ever player to pull on the red jersey of Nottingham Forest, and those who are wrong. The contribution the chubby left-winger made to the club's glory years in the late-1970s should never be underestimated and parallels that of the management of those triumphant times, Brian Clough and Peter Taylor. Yet, without that pair, Robertson would probably have settled into a career with nothing special to relate other than being a haphazardly creative central midfielder. Robertson had joined Forest in May 1970 when 17, and then spent five sporadic seasons in and out of the team. When Clough joined the club as manager in January 1975 Robertson was transfer-listed and seemingly on his way out of the City Ground, but Clough detected something worth preserving within Robertson's scruffy persona and gave the young Scot a chance to prove himself. It wasn't until 1976 though that the crucial moment came when Clough handed Robertson the number 11 shirt and ordered him into the unfamiliar territory of the left wing. What happened next? Promotion, the league title, two League Cups and two European Cups. While, of course, all this silverware was not solely down to Robertson (several other players and in particular, Peter Shilton and Kenny Burns can lay claim to having lent a helping hand or foot), the newly-born left-winger contributed in one way or another to the vast majority of Forest's goals over this period. He could ghost past players and deliver the ball with fiendish precision, scored many goals himself and despatched penalties with ruthless efficiency, and was also remarkable consistent, at one stage appearing in 243 consecutive games. The mantra became "stop Robertson and you stop Forest" but that simply didn't work as if you put two men on him it simply opened up more space for the rest of the Forest team to work in. Robertson graced Forest's left wing for years until a disputed transfer to Derby County in 1983 while between contracts in a move that ended the relationship between Clough and Taylor. Clough bought him back in 1985 for a final swansong, but approaching 33, the old twinkling magic had mostly deserted Robertson's boots and he was released at the end of the 1985/86 season. In 1972 any fan would have been shot for claiming any better player than Ian Storey-Moore would grace Forest's number 11 shirt, but then along came "Robbo".

YOUNG GUNS

The youngest players to make their debut for Forest. Only players whose birthdates are known and confirmed are included:

1   Steve Burke ....16 years 21 days ....(20th Oct v Ayr United)
2   Lee Glover ....16 years 209 days ....(19th Nov 1986 v Bradford)
3   Craig Westcarr.......16 years 257 days ....(13th Oct 2001 v Burnley)
4   Gary Mills...............16 years 302 days ....(9th Sep 1978 v Arsenal)
5   Bryn Gunn..............17 years 5 days .... (27th Aug 1975 v Rotherham)
6   David Pleat.............17 years 32 days ....(17th Feb 1963 v Cardiff)
7   Ashley Hunt ....17 years 71 days ....(4th Feb 1939 v Tranmere)
8   Martin Earp...........17 years 133 days (18th Jan 1890 v Derby Midland)
9   Sammy Chapman.17 years 153 days ....(18th Jan 1964 v Stoke)
10 Felix Bastians..........17 years 161 days ....(18th Oct 2005 v Woking)

Craig Westcarr holds the record for the youngest league debutant. Gary Mills holds the record for the youngest full debutant. David Pleat also holds the record for the youngest player ever to score for Forest, as he scored on his debut against Cardiff City.

OI! GRANDAD!

The oldest players to play for Forest. Again, only players with confirmed birthdates are included:

1   Dave Beasant ....42 years 47 days.......... (6th May 2001 v Tranmere)
2   Sam Hardy.............41 years 38 days...........(4th Oct 1924 v Newcastle)
3   Freddie Scott.........39 years 344 days ....(15th Sep 1956 v Rotherham)
4   Harry Walker........38 years 267 days .... (12th Feb 1955 v Notts Co)
5   Des Walker ....38 years 254 days..............(7th Aug 2004 v Wigan)
6   Horace Gager ....38 years 45 days ......(12th Mar 1955 v Plymouth)
7   Bob Wallace..........37 years 360 days ....(17th Jan 1930 v Stoke)
8   Jack Hutchinson... 37 years 110 days ....(20th Sep 1958 v Bolton)
9   Moreno Mannini . 37 years 100 days (14th Nov 1999 v Huddersfield)
10 Bobby McKinlay.. 37 years 35 days ......(15th Nov 1969 v Newcastle)

Dave Beasant also holds the record as Forest's oldest debutant, making his bow against Oxford United on 23rd August 1997 at the age of 38 years and 156 days.

LIKE A FINE WINE... FOREST'S OLDEST-EVER PLAYER DAVE BEASANT

FOREST'S SEASON-BY-SEASON RECORD

Season	Division	Tier	P	W	D	L	F	A	Pts	Pos
1892/93	First Division	1	30	10	8	12	48	52	28	10th
1893/94	First Division	1	30	14	4	12	57	48	32	7th
1894/95	First Division	1	30	13	5	12	50	56	31	7th
1895/96	First Division	1	30	11	3	16	42	57	25	13th
1896/97	First Division	1	30	9	8	13	44	49	26	11th
1897/98	First Division	1	30	11	9	10	47	49	31	8th
1898/99	First Division	1	34	11	11	12	42	42	33	11th
1899/00	First Division	1	34	13	8	13	56	55	34	8th
1900/01	First Division	1	34	16	7	11	53	36	39	4th
1901/02	First Division	1	34	13	9	12	43	43	35	5th
1902/03	First Division	1	34	14	7	13	49	47	35	10th
1903/04	First Division	1	34	11	9	14	57	57	31	9th
1904/05	First Division	1	34	9	7	18	40	61	25	16th
1905/06	First Division	1	38	13	5	20	58	79	31	19th
1906/07	Second Division	2	38	28	4	6	74	36	60	1st
1907/08	First Division	1	38	13	11	14	59	62	37	9th
1908/09	First Division	1	38	14	8	16	66	57	36	14th
1909/10	First Division	1	38	11	11	16	54	72	33	14th
1910/11	First Division	1	38	9	7	22	55	75	25	20th
1911/12	Second Division	2	38	13	7	18	46	48	33	15th
1912/13	Second Division	2	38	12	8	18	58	59	32	17th
1913/14	Second Division	2	38	7	9	22	37	76	23	20th
1914/15	Second Division	2	38	10	9	19	43	77	29	18th
1919/20	Second Division	2	42	11	9	22	43	73	31	18th
1920/21	Second Division	2	42	12	12	18	48	55	36	18th
1921/22	Second Division	2	42	22	12	8	51	30	56	1st
1922/23	First Division	1	42	13	8	21	41	70	34	20th
1923/24	First Division	1	42	10	12	20	42	64	32	20th
1924/25	First Division	1	42	6	12	24	29	65	24	22nd
1925/26	Second Division	2	42	14	8	20	51	73	36	17th
1926/27	Second Division	2	42	18	14	10	80	55	50	5th
1927/28	Second Division	2	42	15	10	17	83	84	40	10th
1928/29	Second Division	2	42	15	12	15	71	70	42	11th
1929/30	Second Division	2	42	13	15	14	55	69	41	10th
1930/31	Second Division	2	42	14	9	19	80	85	37	17th
1931/32	Second Division	2	42	16	10	16	77	72	42	11th
1932/33	Second Division	2	42	17	15	10	67	59	49	5th
1933/34	Second Division	2	42	13	9	20	73	74	35	17th

Season	Division	Tier	P	W	D	L	F	A	Pts	Pos
1934/35	Second Division	2	42	17	8	17	76	70	42	9th
1935/36	Second Division	2	42	12	11	19	69	76	35	19th
1936/37	Second Division	2	42	12	10	20	68	90	34	18th
1937/38	Second Division	2	42	14	8	20	47	60	36	20th
1938/39	Second Division	2	42	10	11	21	49	82	31	20th
1946/47	Second Division	2	42	15	10	17	69	74	40	11th
1947/48	Second Division	2	42	12	11	19	54	60	35	19th
1948/49	Second Division	2	42	14	7	21	50	54	35	21st
1949/50	Third Division (S)	3	42	20	9	13	67	39	49	4th
1950/51	Third Division (S)	3	46	30	10	6	110	40	70	1st
1951/52	Second Division	2	42	18	13	11	77	62	49	4th
1952/53	Second Division	2	42	18	8	16	77	67	44	7th
1953/54	Second Division	2	42	20	12	10	86	59	52	4th
1954/55	Second Division	2	42	16	7	19	58	62	39	15th
1955/56	Second Division	2	42	19	9	14	68	63	47	7th
1956/57	Second Division	2	42	22	10	10	94	55	54	2nd
1957/58	First Division	1	42	16	10	16	69	63	42	10th
1958/59	First Division	1	42	17	6	19	71	74	40	13th
1959/60	First Division	1	42	13	9	20	50	74	35	20th
1960/61	First Division	1	42	14	9	19	62	78	37	14th
1961/62	First Division	1	42	13	10	19	63	79	36	19th
1962/63	First Division	1	42	17	10	15	67	69	44	9th
1963/64	First Division	1	42	16	9	17	64	68	41	13th
1964/65	First Division	1	42	17	13	12	71	67	47	5th
1965/66	First Division	1	42	14	8	20	56	72	36	18th
1966/67	First Division	1	42	23	10	9	64	41	56	2nd
1967/68	First Division	1	42	14	11	17	52	64	39	11th
1968/69	First Division	1	42	10	13	19	45	57	33	18th
1969/70	First Division	1	42	10	18	14	50	71	38	15th
1970/71	First Division	1	42	14	8	20	42	61	36	16th
1971/72	First Division	1	42	8	9	25	47	81	25	21st
1972/73	Second Division	2	42	14	12	16	47	52	40	14th
1973/74	Second Division	2	42	15	15	12	57	43	45	7th
1974/75	Second Division	2	42	12	14	16	43	55	38	16th
1975/76	Second Division	2	42	17	12	13	55	40	46	8th
1976/77	Second Division	2	42	21	10	11	77	43	52	3rd
1977/78	First Division	1	42	25	14	3	69	24	64	1st
1978/79	First Division	1	42	21	18	3	61	26	60	2nd
1979/80	First Division	1	42	20	8	14	63	43	48	5th
1980/81	First Division	1	42	19	12	11	62	44	50	7th

Season	Division	Tier	P	W	D	L	F	A	Pts	Pos
1981/82	First Division	1	42	15	12	15	42	48	57	12th
1982/83	First Division	1	42	20	9	13	62	50	69	5th
1983/84	First Division	1	42	22	8	12	76	45	74	3rd
1984/85	First Division	1	42	19	7	16	56	48	64	9th
1985/86	First Division	1	42	19	11	12	69	53	68	8th
1986/87	First Division	1	42	18	11	13	64	51	65	8th
1987/88	First Division	1	40	20	13	7	67	39	73	3rd
1988/89	First Division	1	38	17	13	8	64	43	64	3rd
1989/90	First Division	1	38	15	9	14	55	47	54	9th
1990/91	First Division	1	38	14	12	12	65	50	54	8th
1991/92	First Division	1	42	16	11	15	60	58	59	8th
1992/93	Premiership	1	42	10	10	22	41	62	40	22nd
1993/94	First Division	2	46	23	14	9	74	49	83	2nd
1994/95	Premiership	1	42	22	11	9	72	43	77	3rd
1995/96	Premiership	1	38	15	13	10	50	54	58	9th
1996/97	Premiership	1	38	6	16	16	31	59	34	20th
1997/98	First Division	2	46	28	10	8	82	42	94	1st
1998/99	Premiership	1	38	7	9	22	35	69	30	20th
1999/00	First Division	2	46	14	14	18	53	55	56	14th
2000/01	First Division	2	46	20	8	18	55	53	68	11th
2001/02	First Division	2	46	12	18	16	50	51	54	16th
2002/03	First Division*	2	46	20	14	12	82	50	74	6th
2003/04	First Division	2	46	15	15	16	61	58	60	14th
2004/05	Championship	2	46	9	17	20	42	66	44	23rd
2005/06	League 1	3	46	19	12	15	67	52	69	7th
2006/07	League 1*	3	46	23	13	10	65	41	82	4th
2007/08	League 1	3	46	22	16	8	64	32	82	2nd
2008/09	Championship	2	46	13	14	19	50	65	53	19th
2009/10	Championship*	2	46	22	13	11	65	40	79	3rd
2010/11	Championship*	2	46	20	15	11	69	50	75	6th
2011/12	Championship	2	46	14	8	24	48	63	50	19th

*qualified for end of season play-offs

Two points for a win until 1980/81, then three points for a win onwards. Football League and Premiership seasons only. Forest also played three seasons in the Football Alliance, also known as the Northern Alliance, finishing 11th out of 12 teams in 1889/90, fifth out of 12 teams in 1890/91, and first out of 12 teams in 1891/92, the final season of the Alliance.

PLAY-OFF WOES

In 1986, the Football League introduced play-offs in the bottom three tiers to give more teams something to look forward to at the end of the season. Forest, at the time an established top flight side, had no interest, and hoped never to have any, but following the club's initial departure from the Premiership in 1993 they have competed in the play-offs four times and experienced heartbreak on each occasion. In 2002 Paul Hart's youthful squad finished sixth and earned a tie against Sheffield United. The first leg finished 1-1 but importantly, Michael Dawson was sent off towards the end and banned from the return leg. This barely seemed to matter as Forest took a 2-0 lead at Bramall Lane, only for United to pull it back to 2-2 and force extra time. The Blades then led 4-2 and although Forest made it 4-3 with seconds left it was United who went through to the final, where they lost 3-0 to Wolves. In 2007 Forest had at least one foot in the League 1 final when they came back from Yeovil Town's Huish Park with a 2-0 first leg lead. In the second leg at the City Ground, Yeovil produced a remarkable turnaround when they levelled matters in normal time with the score at 3-1. Yeovil then went 4-1 up in extra time, but even though Gary Holt tugged Forest back to level on aggregate, future Red Arron Davies hit the winner to give Yeovil a 5-2 win on the night and a 5-4 victory overall. Fast forward to 2010 when Forest finished third in the Championship and were favourites to return to the top flight. Forest lost the first leg 2-1 at Blackpool but Rob Earnshaw levelled the tie in the second. DJ Campbell and Earnshaw (again) made it 3-3 overall, but then Forest completely collapsed, allowing Blackpool three goals in eight minutes to go 6-4 up. A late Dele Adebola strike made no difference as Blackpool reached the final, where they beat Cardiff City. A year later Forest made the play-offs again but were underdogs against Swansea City. The first leg began well when Swansea's Neil Taylor was sent off inside two minutes, but the Reds couldn't make the advantage work for them and it ended 0-0. In the second leg Forest pulled off one of their best performances of the season but still went down 3-1, with Swansea's last goal a long punt from Darren Pratley after Lee Camp had gone up for a corner.

FOREST IN EUROPE

* Denotes a game settled on the away goals rule

1961/62 Inter-Cities Fairs Cup

FIRST ROUND v Valencia (Spain) LOST 7-1. First leg (A) L 2-0 (Waldo 15, 40); second leg (H) L 5-1 (Cobb 53: Waldo 11, 13, Núñez 30, 49, 68).

1967/68 Inter-Cities Fairs Cup

FIRST ROUND v Eintracht Frankfurt (West Germany) WON 5-0. First leg (A) W 1-0 (Baker 10); second leg (A) W 4-0 (Baker 13, 35, Chapman 47, Lyons 73).
SECOND ROUND v FC Zürich (Switzerland) LOST 2-2*. First leg (H) W 2-1 (Newton 49, Storey-Moore 72 penalty; Künzli 58); second leg (A) L 1-0 (Winiger 70).

1978/79 European Cup

FIRST ROUND v Liverpool WON 2-0. First leg (H) W 2-0 (Birtles 26, Barrett 87); second leg (A) D 0-0.
SECOND ROUND v AEK Athens (Greece) WON 7-2. First leg (A) W 2-1 (McGovern 10, Birtles 45; Mitropoulos 59 penalty); second leg (H) W 5-1 (Needham 12, Woodcock 35, Anderson 40, Birtles 66, 72; Bajevic 50).
QUARTER-FINAL v Grasshoppers (Switzerland) WON 5-2. First leg (H) W 4-1 (Birtles 31, Robertson 47 penalty, Gemmill 87, Lloyd 89; Sulser 11); second leg D 1-1 (O'Neill 38; Sulser 33 penalty).
SEMI-FINAL v FC Köln (West Germany) W 4-3. First leg (H) D 3-3 (Birtles 28, Bowyer 53, Robertson 63; van Gool 6, Müller 20, Okudera 85); second leg (A) W 1-0 (Bowyer 65).
FINAL v Malmö FF (Sweden) W 1-0 (Francis 45) at Olympiastadion (Munich).

1979 European Super Cup

FINAL v Barcelona (Spain) WON 2-1. First leg (H) (George 9); second leg (A) D 1-1 (Burns 42; Roberto 25 pen).

1979/80 European Cup

FIRST ROUND v Östers IF (Sweden) WON 3-1. First leg (H) W 2-0 (Bowyer 63, 73); second leg (A) D 1-1 (Woodcock 79; Nordgren 52).

SECOND ROUND v Arges Pitesti (Romania) WON 4-1. First leg (H) W 2-0 (Woodcock 12, Birtles 16); second leg (A) W 2-1 (Bowyer 5, Birtles 23; Barbulescu 60 penalty).

QUARTER-FINAL v Dynamo Berlin (East Germany) WON 3-2. First leg (H) L 1-0 (Riediger 63); second leg (A) W 3-1 (Francis 15, 35, Robertson 39 penalty; Terletzki 49 penalty).

SEMI-FINAL v Ajax (Netherlands) WON 2-1. First leg (H) W 2-0 (Francis 22, Robertson 61 penalty); second leg (A) L 0-1 (Lerby 65).

FINAL v Hamburg (West Germany) WON 1-0 (Robertson 19) at Bernabeu Stadium (Madrid).

1980 European Super Cup

FINAL v Valencia (Spain) LOST 2-2*. First leg (H) W 2-1 (Bowyer 57, 89; Felman 47); second leg L 1-0 (Morena 51).

1980/81 European Cup

FIRST ROUND v CSKA Sofia (Bulgaria) LOST 2-0. First leg (A) L 1-0 (Yonchev 70); second leg (H) L 1-0 (Kerimov 34).

1983/84 UEFA Cup

FIRST ROUND v FC Vorwärts (East Germany) WON 3-0. First leg (H) W 2-0 (Wallace 16, Hodge 61); second leg (A) W 1-0 (Bowyer 66).

SECOND ROUND v PSV Eindhoven (Netherlands) WON 3-1. First leg (A) W 2-1 (Davenport 51, Walsh 89 penalty; Koolhof 84 penalty); second leg (H) W 1-0 (Davenport 55).

THIRD ROUND v Celtic WON 2-1. First leg (H) D 0-0; second leg (A) W 2-1 (Hodge 53, Walsh 74; MacLeod 79).

QUARTER-FINAL v SK Sturm Graz (Austria) WON 2-1. First leg (H) W 1-0 (Hart 70); second leg (A) D 1-1 (Walsh 114 penalty, Bakota 44 penalty).

SEMI-FINAL v Anderlecht (Belgium) LOST 3-2. First leg (H) W 2-0 (Hodge 72, 81); second leg (A) L 3-0 (Scifo 18, Brylle 60 penalty, Vanderycken 88).

1984/85 UEFA Cup

FIRST ROUND v Club Brugge (Belgium) LOST 1-0. First leg (H) D 0-0; second leg (A) L 1-0 (Wellens 89).

1995/96 UEFA Cup

FIRST ROUND v Malmö FF (Sweden) WON 2-2*. First leg (A) L 2-1 (Woan 36; Persson 59, Andersson 72); second leg (H) W 1-0 (Roy 69).
SECOND ROUND v AJ Auxerre (France) WON 1-0. First leg (A) W 1-0 (Stone 23); second leg (H) D 0-0.
THIRD ROUND v Olympique Lyonnais (France) WON 1-0. First leg (H) W 1-0 (McGregor 83); second leg (A) D 0-0.
QUARTER-FINAL v Bayern München (Germany) LOST 7-5. First leg (A) L 2-1 (Chettle 17; Klinsmann 16, Scholl 35); second leg (H) L 5-1 (Stone 85; Ziege 30, Strunz 43, Klinsmann 65, 80, Papin 73).

BARGAIN BUYS #2

He tasted European glory, scored goals aplenty and brought in a net of £948,000 in transfer fees – not bad for a carpet-fitter from Long Eaton. Signed as a winger from Long Eaton United for £2,000 in 1976, Garry Birtles emerged as one of the best strikers of the late-1970s and early-1980s. He was a lethal finisher, had strength and pace and was an excellent header of the ball. He superseded Peter Withe in the Forest side and scored 26 goals in his first full season. Manchester United offered £1.25m for him in October 1980 and Birtles went to Old Trafford, but was back at Forest two years later after an infamously torrid time with United in which he failed to score for an entire year. He had obviously left his scoring boots at the City Ground as he continued where he left off at Forest, even doubling as a centre-half on occasions. There came a major shock when Birtles was handed a free transfer at the end of the 1986/87 season despite finishing as joint leading goalscorer. He nipped over the Trent to join County, more recognised there as a centre-half than striker as his career tailed off, then ended up at Grimsby Town. Birtles now works in the media.

EIGHT IN A ROW

The record for scoring in consecutive league games for Forest stands at eight and is shared between Forest greats Grenville Morris and Dave "Boy" Martin. Morris just has the edge in scoring 11 goals in his run, between 20th December 1902 and 31st January 1903. Martin managed ten between 5th September and 10th October 1936. Morris' consecutive run came in the middle of his finest-ever goalscoring sequence in which he scored 16 goals in 14 games.

DOWN ARGENTINE WAY

In 1905, Forest became pioneers of English football when they were invited by the Argentinian FA to tour Argentina and Uruguay for the princely sum of £200 (and expenses). A party of 13 players, plus vice-president Harry Radford and secretary/manager Harry Haslam, embarked from Southampton and undertook a gruelling three-week journey via steamer to almost the other side of the world. To keep fit during the voyage, the players ran laps of the ship and played deck cricket. South American football was still finding its feet at the time so Forest were a little unsure as to the standard of opposition they would be facing, but they soon found out as they breezed past their opening opponents, Uruguayan side Penarol, 6-1, with Alf Spouncer helping himself to a hat-trick. From then on, Forest enjoyed themselves with commanding victory following commanding victory. Five days after beating Penarol the Reds crossed the border to Rosario who they beat 5-0, then it was on to Buenos Aires where they hammered Belgrano 7-0, a game in which Billy Shearman hit four. Next, Forest took on Britanicos, a club formed by former British patriots, and triumphed 13-1, with Shearman scoring four again and Fred Lessons weighing in with the same total. Rosario then had another go, and lost 6-0, followed by Alumni, who were beaten 6-1. Next it was the turn of Argentinos, who went down 5-0, and finally a representative Argentinian League side made up of players from all the top sides were soundly slaughtered 9-1 in front of 10,000 supporters. Forest then returned home with Haslam declaring that Argentine football was on a par with the English Second Division, and that the sport had a very bright future there. Forest had scored 57 goals with only three in reply, this despite allowing their star inside-forward and leading goal-getter, Grenville Morris, to remain at home. As an aside, the founding president of Independiente, Aristides Langona, attended the match between Forest and Alumni and so impressed was he by the Reds, that he changed his club's usual colours of Blackburn Rovers-style blue and white halved shirts to match those of Forest. Independiente went on to become one of Argentina's premier sides, winning their national championship 14 times and the Copa Libertadores seven times, wearing red shirts from 1908 onwards.

THE RECORD HOLDERS #2

Most Goals - Grenville Morris (217, 1898-1912)

Born Arthur Grenville Morris in Builth Wells, Wales on 13th April 1887, Morris came to be known as The Prince of the Inside-Lefts and as one of the greatest forwards of his generation. He began his career in local league football with Builth Town and Aberystwyth Town before moving to Swindon Town in early-1897. He played 50 games for the Robins, and his 44 goals alerted Forest – who had just added to their coffers with the 1898 FA Cup win – to his talents, and they splashed out £200 for him. It was a magnificent signing, as Morris soon became Forest's best forward since the days of Sam Widdowson, Tinsley Lindley and latterly, Sandy Higgins. In his 15 years at Forest, Morris scored a total of 217 goals in all competitions, with 199 being attributed to him in league football (statistics were not routinely kept at the time so it was only later in history that it became known that Morris had missed the magic 200 figure by one). He formed a deadly partnership for a short spell with Enoch West before the latter's transfer to Manchester United. Morris was a regular for Wales throughout his career, although as there were only an average of three internationals each year, he only won 21 caps (scoring nine times). Morris retired from football just prior to the outbreak of the First World War. He lived until he was 82, and was still alive to see Forest win the FA Cup at Wembley in 1959.

FOREST'S TOP TEN GOALSCORERS

1   Grenville Morris (1898-1912, 199 league).................................. 217
2   Nigel Clough (1984-93, 1996-97, 102 league) 131
3   Wally Ardron (1949-55, 123 league).. 124
4   Johnny Dent (1926-36, 119 league) 122
5   Ian Storey-Moore (1962-71, 105 league)................................... 118
6   Enoch West (1905-09, 93 league) 100
7= Garry Birtles (1976-80, 1982-86, 70 league) 96
7= Ian Bowyer (1973-80, 1981-86, 68 league).................................. 96
9   John Robertson (1970-82, 1985-86, 61 league).......................... 95
10 Tommy Wilson (1951-60, 75 league) 89

NUMBER TWELVE IS...

Garath McCleary. Purely on the basis of holding the record number of substitute appearances for the club, surpassing the previous holder, striker Nathan Tyson, in 2011. McCleary is a hark back to the bargain buy days of Brian Clough when he snapped the likes of Gary Crosby and Ian Woan up from non-league obscurity and moulded them into first team regulars. The right-winger found himself on Colin Calderwood's radar in 2007 after a year at Bromley as a winger and striker and after a successful trial, signed for the club in January 2008. His appearances in the side remained sporadic for several seasons, as neither Calderwood nor his successor, Billy Davies, allowed McCleary a run in the starting XI, hence the Oxford-born player instead amassing a sizeable number of appearances from the bench. McCleary improved as a player in decent chunks but it still wasn't until 2011, and the appointment of Steve Cotterill as boss, that the winger became a regular in the side, and he repaid Cotterill's faith in him with a series of dazzling displays, none more so than the 7-3 destruction of Leeds United at Elland Road in March 2012 in which McCleary scored four goals. McCleary's 2011/12 ended prematurely through injury as Forest spluttered into survival, but he still finished as the club's top scorer with nine goals before joining Reading, newly promoted to the Premiership.

SPONSORED

When the Football League first allowed shirt sponsorship in 1980 (but not on TV), Nottingham Forest, the then European champions, were one of the hottest attractions to have a company's name emblazoned across their shirts. It was no surprise then that a two-year deal was signed with the giant Japanese electronic firm Panasonic. This was followed for a season in 1983/84 when the US clothing company Wrangler became the club's main sponsors. In 1984 a 13-year association with breweries began, starting with Skol (1984-86), then local brands Home Ales (1986-87) and Shipstones (1987-91) and finally the Canadian company Labatt (1992-97). As Forest began to struggle financially it seemed appropriate that the next two sponsors were both based in financial markets, namely the insurance company Pinnacle Insurance (1997-2003) and the Nottingham-based UK arm of the giant American financial corporation Capital One. Bookmakers Victor Chandler took over from Capital One in 2009, and were replaced by Nottingham-based John Pye & Sons Auctioneers in 2012.

DURING THE WAR

Forest's complete league record shows two gaps where league football was suspended due to war, but as the continuation of the sport was deemed good for public morale, Forest, as did most league sides, maintained sides in regional competitions. In 1915/16 Forest won the Midland Section comprising of 14 teams, then a further subsidiary competition between themselves, Notts County, Leicester City, Stoke City, Derby County and Chesterfield. The 1916/17 season was not as successful, as Forest finished sixth in the Principal Competition (which was won by Leeds City) of 16 teams, but then 13th in the six-game Subsidiary Competition. The next season saw the same format with Forest finishing fifth out of 15 teams, then fourth from bottom. In 1918/19, however, Forest were effectively crowned league champions, as having won the Midland Section they then defeated Everton (champions of the Northern Section) in a two-legged play-off. The next time competition was suspended, three games into the 1939/40 season, Forest were entered into an 11-team East Midlands League and finished next to bottom. Wartime football during the Second World War was a far more haphazard affair with no guarantee of fixtures being completed and clubs playing when and if they could. In 1940/41 Forest finished 28th out of 34 in the South Regional League, although there were huge discrepancies in the amount of games teams played (Coventry only managed ten, for example, while Stoke played 36) and teams were ranked on goal average. In 1940/41 Forest failed to qualify for the league table having played only 16 of the 18 games required. By the 1942/43 season things had begun to become a little more structured and a massive 48-team Football League North competition had teams playing 18 games. Forest finished 31st, then 19th in the additional League Cup competition. This format continued for 1943/44, with Forest finishing 26th out of 51 in the First Championship, 42nd out of 60 for the Second Championship but then failing to qualify for the League Cup. It was much the same for 1944/45, with final placings of 40th out of 54, 16th out of 56 (in a competition won by the giants of Bath City) and again failing to qualify for the League Cup. In 1945/46, with hostilities reaching a conclusion, the Football League was confident enough to organise a proper competition of 22 sides, and Forest finished 15th in League South.

CAUGHT SHORT(S)

For a while in their early years, Forest played in red shirts and blue shorts, but soon reverted to the familiar white-shorted kit that prevails to this day. However, on one occasion, Forest returned to their previous red and blue combination. On 6th October 1982, Forest took on West Brom at the City Ground in the League Cup, a game that they won 6-1. The Baggies wore their usual dark blue and white striped shirts but with dark blue shorts. Three days later Forest journeyed to the Hawthorns for a league game, assuming West Brom would play in the same kit, but the Baggies insisted on playing in their usual kit of striped shirts with white shorts. Forest hadn't brought their usual red shorts that they used whenever there was such a colour clash. Fortunately, the supporters were spared the sight of the Forest team running around in jockstraps, as Albion lent them a kit's-worth of dark blue shorts.

COME ON YOU...REDS...?

During wartime football, while most teams only retained a slight core of their own players, fixtures could only be fulfilled by the use of "guest" players from other teams, who were stationed or living nearby. On 20th September 1941, Forest travelled to Northampton for a game against the Cobblers and fielded the following side: Harry Riley (FOREST), Jack Challinor (Stoke City), Jock Kirton (Stoke City), Bob Iverson (Aston Villa), George Mason (Coventry City), Les Jones (Arsenal), Frank Broome (Aston Villa), Harry Smith (Fulham), Bill Hullett (Manchester United), Joe Meek (Bradford) and Jack Ward (FOREST). Forest lost the game 4-3 with Hullett, who would join the Reds for a brief spell after the war, scoring twice.

DAMN FOREIGNERS

The Reds' proud record of never losing to foreign opposition came to an end on 23rd May 1950 when Forest went down 5-1 to SV Bremen (now more commonly known as Werder Bremen) in West Germany during the club's post-season tour of western continental Europe, although some sources have Forest down as only losing 2-1. Forest's goal came from a Horace Gager penalty. This run is perhaps not as grand as it first sounds though, as this game was only Forest's 12th against non-British opposition in their history to that point.

NEVER ON A SUNDAY

It is odd to consider now but for well over 100 years Sunday football was a definite no-no. Forest's first-ever Sunday game at the City Ground occurred as recently as 1974 as the FA decided to allow games on a Sunday because of the government-imposed three-day working week and associated power restrictions. On 6th January 1974 Forest hosted Bristol Rovers in the FA Cup third round in front of a season-high crowd of 23,456 spectators and beat them 4-3 thanks to goals by Neil Martin (two), Sammy Chapman and a George Lyall penalty.

THE FIRST £1,000,000 TRANSFER

Famously, Forest became the first English team to pay a fee of £1m for a player in February 1979, England forward Trevor Francis, then of Birmingham City (although Brian Clough later claimed he paid £999,999 to get his man). Less remembered is how protracted a transfer the switch became. Francis arrived at the City Ground on 9th February, and after extended discussions (mainly around Francis' insistence on playing for Detroit Express of the NASL during the summer, with which Clough had issues) Francis signed on the dotted line. On the Saturday, Francis played for the Forest A team against Notts County A, even though, officially, he was still a Birmingham City player as the transfer forms hadn't been signed by anyone from Birmingham. On the Monday, Clough had a change of heart, and negotiations were re-opened and a compromise agreed over Francis' other team, Detroit. Francis was expected to make his Forest debut on the Wednesday at home to Norwich, but the game was postponed, which was fortunate as he remained unregistered as a Forest player. The protracted transfer was finally completed on the 16th, but with Forest without a league game until the 24th, the club hastily agreed to testimonial matches against Exeter City on the 19th and West Brom on the 21st – in both Francis was named as and played as a substitute. On 24th February Francis finally made his Forest bow as a second half substitute for Martin O'Neill, but with Forest playing in the FA Cup the following week against Arsenal and with Francis being cup-tied, he didn't make his full Forest bow until 3rd March at Ipswich Town, replacing Tony Woodcock in the line-up, three weeks after first signing for the club.

HEADS YOU WIN

The amount of silverware amassed by the club between 1976 and 1980 eclipsed every other period in the club's history, but surely there can be none more satisfied than the personal accolade awarded to Forest custodian Peter Shilton, when he won the National Hairdressers' Federation Head of the Year prize in 1978. Shilton's expertly-maintained tight perm saw him walk away with the male version of the award, with BBC newsreader Angela Rippon winning the female title.

BRIAN CLOUGH'S FULL LEAGUE RECORD

Brian Clough's complete season-by-season record while in charge at Nottingham Forest. W% is the percentage of games won out of games played, and Av is the average number of points won per game based on three points for a win. Best performances in a season for each column are asterisked.

Season	P	W	D	L	F	A	W%	Av
1974/75	17	3	8	6	16	23	0.176	1.00
1975/76	42	17	12	13	55	40	0.404	1.50
1976/77	42	21	10	11	77	43	0.500	1.73
1977/78	42	*25	14	*3	69	*24	*0.595	*2.12
1978/79	42	21	*18	*3	61	26	0.500	1.93
1979/80	42	20	8	14	63	43	0.476	1.62
1980/81	42	19	12	11	62	44	0.452	1.64
1981/82	42	15	12	15	42	48	0.357	1.38
1982/83	42	20	9	13	62	50	0.476	1.64
1983/84	42	22	8	12	76	45	0.524	1.76
1984/85	42	19	7	16	56	48	0.452	1.52
1985/86	42	19	11	12	69	53	0.452	1.62
1986/87	42	18	11	13	64	51	0.429	1.55
1987/88	40	20	13	7	67	39	0.500	1.83
1988/89	38	17	13	8	64	43	0.447	1.68
1989/90	38	15	9	14	55	47	0.395	1.42
1990/91	38	14	12	12	65	50	0.368	1.42
1991/92	42	16	11	15	60	58	0.381	1.40
1992/93	42	10	10	22	41	62	0.238	0.95
Totals	759	331	208	220	1124	837	0.436	1.58

WHERE'S THE GOAL?

The Reds have had their fair share of prolific strikers over the years, but they also had plenty of goal-shy forwards. Dean Saunders (five league goals in 39 league starts), Robert Rosario (three in 25), Alex Ingram (three in 27) and Justin Fashanu (three in 31) all commanded hefty fees yet couldn't find the target with the regularity such outlays demanded. Neil Shipperley was another big buy after promotion in 1997/98, but scored once in 13 starts (and eight substitute appearances). Even worse, and far more puzzling, Neil Harris spent just over two years at Forest and scored a single goal in 19 starts and 19 substitute appearances. Harris has, at the time of writing, managed to score 140 goals for the other clubs he has played for. Two youngsters, Colin Hall (two goals in 29 starts, 1967-70) and Alan Buckley (one goal in 16 starts, 1967-73) couldn't bring the promise they had shown at reserve team level to the first team. The king of Forest's goal-shy wonders though must be 1950s terrace boo-boy Arthur Lemon, who was thought by many to be Billy Walker's favourite despite his lack of composure in front of the net. Lemon scored once in 24 games.

WHERE THE STREETS HAVE A NAME

The Forest side of 1987/88 was probably on par with that of 1966/67 in claiming to be Forest's second best ever team below that of the legendary 1977/78 vintage. The home-builders Wimpey decided to honour the 1988 side's achievements in naming five cul-de-sacs that formed part of a new housing development in Beechdale after members of that group of players. Hence Pearce Drive (which was quite appropriate given the power of Psycho's shooting), Clough Court, Chapman Court, Gaynor Court and Webb Road. Sadly, the opening of the estate was marred by Neil Webb's defection to Old Trafford, although happily Wimpey decided against moving that section of the estate to Manchester.

THE ULTIMATE, ULTIMATE FOREST TEAM

1: Brian Rice. 2: Brian Rice. 3: Brian Rice. 4: Brian Rice. 5: Brian Rice. 6: Brian Rice. 7: Brian Rice. 8: Brian Rice. 9: Brian Rice. 10: Brian Rice. 11: Brian Rice. 12: Brian Rice. We all, of course, live in a world of Brian Rice.